Windows of Heaven

Windows of Heaven

By

GLENN CLARK

Graphic editing and all photographs
unless otherwise stated

by

LUCIEN AIGNER

Published by
ARTHUR JAMES
The Drift, Evesham, Worcs.

First published in England 1955
Reprinted 1956
Reprinted 1959

MADE AND PRINTED IN GREAT BRITAIN BY PURNELL AND SONS, LTD
PAULTON (SOMERSET) AND LONDON

CONTENTS

FOREWORD

by

The Bishop of Worcester

THIS is a most inspiring book and for one main reason. It consists of vital passages from Dr. Clark's previous books and is published in the form of daily meditations, combined with a very beautiful series of photographs. This seems to me a wonderful illustration of the title of the book. " Windows of Heaven" seem to be open through these pictures of nature and people and they illumine what is said in the meditations.

Those who have read Glenn Clark's previous writings will recognize that in a rather unique way he is a teacher of prayer, and a teacher who speaks from personal experience, both rich and enriching. He tells us to breathe deeply the beauty and fragrance of God, and let our souls beat with His love. His key-note is " Be still," that we may hear God's voice. The truth of God sparkles through these pages, lifting us up to the " secret place of the Most High."

As we follow these meditations daily, prayer will become as natural as breathing, and we shall reflect the love and joy of Christ's presence. Our own level of prayer will become a life-long experience, deepening as it grows stronger, developing as faith increases, creating a peace of mind and heart that controls our lives.

I would warmly commend this beautifully arranged book to all who would learn to-day the meaning of prayer.

WILLIAM WORCESTER.

Hartlebury Castle,
   Kidderminster,
      Worcestershire.

THE WINDOWS OPEN

by

Glenn Clark

I WAS a child with a child's natural curiosity when I began peeping into the windows of heaven.

The windows opened wide for the first time when my little brother Page died, and for a while I actually practised the presence of God. When I was forty years old my mother died, and then the windows opened so wide that I wrote my discoveries into my first book, *The Soul's Sincere Desire*. When the editor sent me a copy of the jacket I was amazed to read : " This is the personal record of a man who has learned to pray as naturally as to breathe and whose every prayer is answered." Anxious to correct such a statement I started to write to Ellery Sedgwick, but Louise my wife stopped me, saying: " I wouldn't bother, Glenn. I've noticed that ever since your mother died three years ago all of your prayers are answered." And I knew what she meant. It seemed that as soon as my mother stepped into heaven her wishes for me, which had been limited by the inhibitions and tensions of earthly life, were set free and multiplied by Infinity. I had been experiencing such power in prayer as I never dreamed possible before.

★   ★   ★   ★

When Stephen, the martyr, failed to win Saul of Tarsus to Christianity, and was stoned by Saul's men, he died praying, " Lay not this sin to their charge." Almost immediately Saul met Christ on the Damascus Road, and the Christian Church was born.

Jesus said, " Greater works than I have done ye shall do BECAUSE I GO UNTO THE FATHER." And he went on to explain in his own glorious language how the Holy Spirit would come to everyone whose heart was open to God and believing in Jesus Christ His Son.

When friends urged me to assemble the most vital passages from my books and publish them as daily meditations I hesitated because I knew that words alone are inadequate to give us the vision of heaven on earth that I wanted to describe.

And then at one of the Camps Farthest Out[1] I met Lucien Aigner, a professional photographer, who brings to his camera work a spiritual perception. Even to glance at one of his pictures is to be lifted into the higher planes of awareness. I knew he was to be my collaborator.

The matching of meditations with photographs became an adventure for us, in which we let ourselves be carried away on the wings of prayer. I was amazed to discover how much inspired pictures can heighten verbal concepts, giving a stereoscopic or double view into the heart of realities.

We dug deeply into Aigner's rich files and he also collected a few photographs from photographer friends. My friend John Budd supplied us with some views of mountainous terrain which reflect powerfully the handiwork of God.

★   ★   ★   ★

Twenty-five years ago I had a dream, or soul's sincere desire, which has been fulfilled far beyond my capacity to vision. The Camps Farthest Out now number almost fifty in my country alone, and as I go on my travels round the world I take with me that same dream, praying it will be realized in all the nations of the world. The Camps Farthest Out are dedicated to the purpose of discovering the wholeness of that abundant life which Christ promised, that life which is our rightful heritage whenever we dedicate our body, mind and soul completely to God through play, work and worship. Because we believe that the planting of sacred Truths cannot bear much fruit unless the mind and imagination are fertile, we invite our Campers to enter the kindergarten of creativity and discover all the joyous opportunities for normal spiritual expression. And so we sing in rhythm, paint pictures, do sculpturing, and even write poetry as a part of our regular Camp programme. For the highest art of life is a living prayer, a continual, dynamic and whole-souled communion with God and man in His image, through Jesus Christ.

In closing this introduction I want to share with you a precious blessing in my life. A year after my wife died our two daughters married. Marion,

[1] The secretary of the Camps Farthest Out in Great Britain is Peter S. Hodge, "Glanbrane", 47 Gordon Avenue, Stanmore, Middx.

the younger, had two children, but doctors told Helen May she could never have babies of her own. Marion and I prayed together about this and presently word came that Helen May and Kermit expected their first child, to be born the middle of July. July came and went, and on August 4 I received a telegram: " Little Glenn just arrived." Two years later Helen May was expecting a second child, this one due at the end of August. But on August 4 there was a telegram: " Gordon just arrived." When the editor was discussing a publishing date for this book, he remarked, " August 4 will be about the right time." Now I will tell you that August 4 was the birthday of my wife, Louise. And I just know that God let her pick, from all that wonderful assortment of babies in heaven, the two which were best for Helen May and Kermit. And I know also that this book is coming to birth because God planned to open some Windows of Heaven through its pages.

> And prove me now herewith, saith the Lord of hosts, if I will not open you the windows of heaven, and pour you out a blessing, that there shall not be room enough to receive it. (Malachi 3 : 10)

Windows of Heaven

In the Beginning God

HAVE you ever wondered what the world looked like when it was just a vast unfinished place—teeming and stewing, only half guessing what it was to be? If you want to know how things looked during that first half-week of Creation, look upon the sea!

Here, on the island of my soul, I have a little dream shack by the water, and I wait for people like you to come and worship here with me. But when those people who blunder through all the beautiful places of the earth try to come and make a display of their gold, setting up big houses and calling menservants and maidservants, I tell them this heaven is my own and it may not be bought.

I shall always keep my temple above the restless waves—for pure joys. Just a little rocky island balanced up against a dusty continent, and guarded —as with a flaming sword—by the four seasons. To all who pass, the sea cries out: " Except ye be as little children, ye shall not enter here!" But the ones like you and me who come to worship may have all the room we need to breathe and move and run and leap—to become pure and strong and free!

And these silent, bleak and mighty rocks, this Home of stars and snows, with winds playing in the grasses, and waters circling round it tolling . . . tolling at its doors—this is kept for God, and you and me.

When it is time to go back to the continent we shall understand the rhythms of the universe, of tide and gravity, of strength and release. We shall be a part of all the universal forces, moving with strange new power and ease. And men with their fortunes and men with their laws will be grasping at *little* things.

> Lay not up for yourselves treasures upon earth, where moth and rust doth corrupt, and where thieves break through and steal: But lay up for yourselves treasures in heaven, where neither moth nor rust doth corrupt, and where thieves do not break through nor steal. (Matthew 6 : 19–20)

Homesick ?

ALL the men and women or boys and girls who have found their way to me seeking help suffered from exactly the same ailment. And that is Homesickness. Homesickness is merely a heartsickness that arises whenever we become conscious of separation from the source of life. All of us at some time experience this consciousness, and call it sin, misfortune or sickness. But whatever the name, the problem is the same, for we are in hell. Old Sam Johnson was right when he defined hell as " a place of separate souls."

Jesus came as a Good Shepherd to seek and to save those who have become separated, or lost. And He leads through green pastures and beside still waters until we are safely Home.

The mother hen, one of the humblest feathered creatures of our common life, symbolizes perfect sheltering love. For she is both mother and habitation for her little ones. Christ—the perfect panacea for Homesickness—still cries out to our age : " O Jerusalem, Jerusalem . . . how often would I have gathered thy children together, even as a hen gathereth her chickens under her wings, and ye would not!" This yearning to take us Home was expressed again and again. " Come unto me, all ye that are weary and heavy laden, and I will give you rest."

Himself a homeless wanderer, Christ came to prepare homes for us both here and in the hereafter, safe in the Kingdom of Love. The deeper we enter into the sanctuary of His Presence, the more secure we feel. And with the inexpressible joy of that oneness we long to lead others where we have come.

In my Father's house are many mansions : if it were not so, I would have told you. I go to prepare a place for you. And if I go and prepare a place for you, I will come again, and receive you unto myself; that where I am, there ye may be also. (John 14 : 2, 3)

Footprints of God

NEVER be ashamed of asking, seeking and knocking at the storehouse of God's omnipotence! " Faith is the substance of things hoped for and the evidence of things not seen." When we admit our helplessness to meet needs on the human level we are expressing our dependence upon God, and that is the faith that moves mountains.

One way to achieve the awareness which brings heavenly blessings into manifestation upon earth, is to look for the footprints of God in the outer realms about you. Transmute these majestic signs of God's omnipotence through meditation and contemplation into your deepest consciousness. Hold them there, as blueprints of His Creation. Then when you feel His blessing breathed upon you, turn from them with perfect faith that the impression is going to crystallize in new inspirations, selfless deeds, miraculous healings and transformed lives.

Some religious leaders find it difficult to decide where prayer for THINGS of this earth go slithering off into the realms of magic and selfishness, instead of remaining properly under God's control. " Seek ye first the Kingdom of Heaven and its righteousness, and all these things will be added unto you," Jesus promised. And the things to which He referred are those which our souls sincerely desire while we are humbly waiting at the feet of God. In this transformed consciousness we are not selfish nor presumptuous. And when we rise, transformed and incandescent, we shall give Him all of the praise and all of the glory.

> How beautiful upon the mountains are the feet of him that bringeth good tidings, that publisheth peace ; that bringeth good tidings of good, that publisheth salvation ; that saith unto Zion, Thy God reigneth! (Isaiah 52 : 7)

Fifteen Minutes for a New World

WOULD you like to discover that you live in a heavenly, new world ? Give me fifteen minutes of your time every morning for about three months, and although I should hesitate to promise—as might a calisthenics instructor—that you will be " a new man," I can say this : At the end of that time you will discover that you live in a new world.

Begin the fifteen-minute period if possible outdoors, or by a large window. Stand gazing upon the landscape and then up at the sky, stretch your mind and take in the vastness of God. Then feel, as you breathe deeply, the fragrance and beauty of God. Now let your soul beat with His Love.

You will begin to discover that you live in a friendly universe where religion is not something to put on or cast off but where it is a part of life, as blood is part of the body. You will see yourself in a new world where God dwells—not just in churches, expressing His wonders only in rituals—but where He governs every moment in every corner of His Creation. You will discover you are in a world where immortality need not be sought after for some future time because you will know you are immortal now, and God's entire domain with all its goodness and with all its beauty belongs to you now and forever!

Each morning will become for you the beginning of an adventure, full of thrilling opportunities and breath-taking surprises. On any door which seems to be closing you will find a sign which points to another that will open upon vistas beyond all your former imagining. Your Father will be with you everywhere you are, sharing with you, His child, the wealth of the Kingdom of Heaven.

And I saw a new heaven and a new earth : for the first heaven and the first earth were passed away ; and there was no more sea. (Revelation 21 : 1)

Growth is a Continuous Process

WE often have the mistaken idea that education should provide external stimulus that will make inner growth possible. Actually, growth is constant, and the true purpose of education should be to open wider and wider the channels of impression and expression so that the inevitable process of growth may proceed in an orderly and normal fashion.

Great geniuses are not men who received " adequate " formal educations. Edison, Lincoln, Socrates and Shakespeare were fortunate enough to have found freedom to grow great from their own inner Light. The purpose to-day in our educational systems seems to be " learning for earning," as though the mere acquisition of factual knowledge is the key to success in life.

Undoubtedly Christ's disciples were uncouth and unlettered at the time He chose them to follow Him. Yet how many of us are worthy to be called the " light of the world " and " fishers of men " ? How many of us have been educated to be the " Sons of God " ?

When we return to a study of the beatitudes of the Sermon on the Mount we discover that eternal verities are not to be measured with mental reasonings. If our whole educational system could be geared to teach us to live as sons of God, debate and rationalization would be replaced with faith that moves mountains of fear and hate. Then indeed would peace reign in the hearts of men. So, why do we wait while men destroy each other with the implements of Mind ?

O Master, we would hear Thy call, " Come follow," and drop the little, idle efforts for so-called civilization to go along the Way which Thou hast trod before us. Though it lead us into shadows of death, or into green pastures, we are Thy servants, prepared to live for Thine eternal purposes in Jesus' name. Amen.

> My doctrine is not mine, but his that sent me. If any man will do his will, he shall know of the doctrine, whether it be of God, or whether I speak of myself. He that speaketh of himself seeketh his own glory : but he that seeketh his glory that sent him, the same is true, and no unrighteousness is in him. (John 7 : 16–18)

You Become What You Adore

EXPERTS on handwriting claim that they can read personality in handwriting. Physiognomists claim that character is revealed in the finer points of skin texture, shape of the nose and set of the jaw. Phrenologists ponder the bumps on the skull. Psychologists claim that personality traits, emotional tendencies and vocational aptitudes can be determined by charts and tests.

But I can show you a simpler way. Tell me what you adore and I will tell you what you are. If you adore gossip your face will wear the mask of a gossip. If you adore money, the pound sign will darken your brow and shape your handclasp. If you adore landscapes and sunsets, tranquillity will be expressed in your gaze and your voice. If you adore Jesus and look up to Him long and often, you will take on the aspects of divinity.

Everyone should read a book about Jesus each year. Better yet, read each day from the gospel records, and come to know the Carpenter of Nazareth. As He becomes real to you through the words He spoke and the report of His deeds on earth, His Presence and Power will be transforming you. You will walk with a new dignity, according to the stature of a child of God. Your motions will be graceful and relaxed because you have yielded to the controlling guidance of that inner Light. Your countenance will radiate Love, and your features will be softened in that radiance until you appear as you really ARE. For the first time you will have become what you *sincerely* adored all the years before.

To whom then will ye liken God ? or what likeness will ye compare unto him ? (Isaiah 40 : 18) Hast thou not known ? hast thou not heard, that the everlasting God, the Lord, the Creator of the ends of the earth, fainteth not, neither is weary ? there is no searching of his understanding. He giveth power to the faint ; and to them that have no might he increaseth strength. Even the youths shall faint and be weary, and the young men shall utterly fall : But they that wait upon the Lord shall renew their strength ; they shall mount up with wings as eagles ; they shall run, and not be weary ; and they shall walk, and not faint. (Isaiah 40 : 28–31)

Be Still and Know

ALMIGHTY FATHER, there is no power on earth but Thine. All our human efforts are vain; what we make to-day is gone to-morrow. Only Thy creations live forever. So help us to be still, that Thy Voice may speak to our needs.

Breathe through us, O Blessed Spirit of the Most High, as we try to drink from the wellsprings of eternal Truth and not from the swamps and fens of the world's dark knowledge. Write Thy statutes on our hearts, plant Thy commandments in our minds. As we lay hold on Thy promises, make us more truly aware of Thy Love for us, and give us an ever-increasing capacity to radiate that Love to all mankind.

We thank Thee, Our Heavenly Father, that we live in a world where Light controls life, and where darkness is but a seeming absence of light. Help us to keep our eyes upon the sunshine and not upon the shadows, upon the realities of the Kingdom and not upon the counterfeits of the Wilderness. Oh, that men would praise Thee more for Thy goodness and for Thy wonderful works! Now let us dream Thy dreams and vision Thy visions, in Jesus' name. Amen.

> He that dwelleth in the secret place of the most High shall abide under the shadow of the Almighty. I will say of the Lord, He is my refuge and my fortress: my God; in him will I trust. Surely he shall deliver thee from the snare of the fowler, and from the noisome pestilence. He shall cover thee with his feathers, and under his wings shalt thou trust: his truth shall be thy shield and buckler. Thou shalt not be afraid for the terror by night; nor for the arrow that flieth by day; nor for the pestilence that walketh in darkness; nor for the destruction that wasteth at noonday. A thousand shall fall at thy side, and ten thousand at thy right hand; but it shall not come nigh thee. (Psalm 91 : 1–7)

A Living Prayer

THERE are times when the world seems to be whirling through dark clouds and the situations in which we find ourselves from day to day are increasingly depressing. At such times I find it is necessary to rise before dawn and go up into the mountain, figuratively speaking, to pray alone. Never have the mists remained when I went into my closet for prayer and meditation, whether early or late.

But the highest art of living consists of making prayer such a natural and continual expression toward God that it works itself into the muscles, and the mind processes, then every act of our daily lives reflects the Love and Joy of Christ's presence. Each day is no longer a fast filled with fear but a feast filled with faith. There is no more monotony, for we live life as a poem or sonata in which every need harmonizes or synchronizes with its perfect fulfilment. To see in a sparrow's fall, or the closing of a door, or the change of a season a part of the rhythm of eternal things—this lifts prayer above mere words and puts it in our eyes, our ears, our sense of touch. This takes prayer out of the meeting house, and forms, and special days, and fills it with the fragrance of moors, the tang of mountains, the freshness of the seas. This creates the music and the poem in every soul that has eyes to see, and ears to hear the eternal rhythms and harmonies.

So little is accomplished by a flimsy perfunctory five- or ten-minute prayer! But ABSOLUTELY NO EVIL CAN STAND BEFORE A TWENTY-FOUR HOUR, LIVING PRAYER POURING FROM A SURRENDERED SOUL. Everything Jesus had to say about the Kingdom of Heaven can be summed up in these words: Give all that you have and all that you are to the Father.

This is prayer in its highest, most perfect expression. This is the wedding of a soul to Christ. This is the feast of thanksgiving which comes after a season of planting and tilling and gathering in the harvest.

And he said to them all, If any man will come after me, let him deny himself, and take up his cross daily, and follow me. For whosoever will save his life shall lose it: but whosoever will lose his life for my sake, the same shall save it. For what is a man advantaged, if he gain the whole world, and lose himself? (Luke 9 : 23–25)

The Divine Instrument

WHAT would we think of a music dealer who locked up in a dank cell a perfect gramophone upon which had been played a poor record, while he continued to sell the poor record indiscriminately?

Although in a sense we are gramophones, we may choose what we will play: the harmonious music of the spheres, or the discordant sounds of hate and fear. Nevertheless when poor records are played upon a perfect gramophone we must not discard or despise the gramophone itself.

Condemn the sin but never the sinner.

Cultivate the habit of seeing the perfection beneath discord and you will discover what a divine instrument God has designed. The only way to help others to cast off their poor records is to cast off the poor records we have been playing ourselves. Like the prodigal we too must cry out, " I have sinned against heaven, and in thy sight: I am no more worthy to be called thy son." Only thus can we rid ourselves of inharmonies and begin to play the celestial music of the spheres.

Father, take us up the ladders of affection for others, from that first mere tolerance to liking, from selfish attachment into friendship, deepening them into comradeship and finally into the highest spiritual Love. There, freed ourselves from judgment and condemnation toward others, may we free them also to turn within the radius of the perfect circle of Thy everwidening Love. In Jesus' name. Amen.

> The light of the body is the eye: if therefore thine eye be single, thy whole body shall be full of light. But if thine eye be evil, thy whole body shall be full of darkness. If therefore the light that is in thee be darkness, how great is that darkness! (Matthew 6: 22, 23)

Three Levels of Worship

THERE are three levels of worship. Jesus told the Samaritan woman : " Ye worship that which ye know not." Hers was ignorant worship. The Jews said : " We worship that which we know." Theirs was intelligent worship. But the highest level of worship was introduced by Jesus Christ : " The hour cometh and now is, when the true worshippers shall worship the Father in spirit and in truth."

To worship in spirit is to look Upward with love ; to worship in truth is to look Upward with trust. When Peter tried to walk upon the water toward the Master and took his gaze from Jesus' face to look down at the water, he began to sink. To worship in spirit and in truth, then, is to trust God's absolute and infinite loving power.

As spirit is not bound by time or space, neither should we be limited to a certain time or place for worship. Begin every day with a prayer of trust. " Acknowledge him in all thy ways and he shall direct thy paths." Then, whenever problems arise during the day direct your thoughts immediately toward God, in a silent prayer for guidance. You will discover that He was already coming toward you on the water!

So, think of God as ALL-LOVING, ALL-POWERFUL, ABSOLUTELY PERFECT. Think that in Him is no imperfection, no selfishness, no hate, no anger, no unworthiness of any sort. Then, with your gaze steadily fixed upon Him, walk out, innocent and pure, to meet Him face to face. You will feel petty annoyance and prejudice and selfish desire fall away from you like cheap garments you can gladly discard, to take on finer raiment. As you present yourself to your Master, Christ, God the Father will bless you.

> Jesus saith unto him, I am the way, and the truth, and the life : no man cometh unto the Father, but by me. (John 14 : 6)

My Joy I Give Unto You

Joy is like lightning, and he who finds his centre in Joy will run like lightning, for Joy is electric. It fills us with power, from the tiniest brain cell to the tip of the toes.

To enter a contest with the sole purpose or hope of winning kills joy at the start. But if you enter a contest with the purpose of enjoying every part of the competition, your efforts will seem like play, and others with whom you compete will be glad for the inspiration of your presence.

Any activity whose reward seems to lie at the end must be drudgery. For when a thing is ended it is dead ; it belongs to the past. So, give yourself to life, not death! Start all life's races with the intention of enjoying thoroughly all the thrills, from that first crack of the gun to the last burst of effort when you break through the tape. It is exhilarating to move arms and legs, to rise into the air at the jumps, to curve around the track in perfect co-ordination. Oh, run for the love of it! Jump for the joy of it! And no matter how far ahead the other fellow gets, keep this love and joy, carry on at a good swinging pace, AND YOU WILL GET THERE.

To pray effectively we need joy, which means that we have to drop all fear and cringing at the start. God chose the umpire, gave us the power, set all the goals, and watches over us constantly. So, lift up your head and be glad!

Thine, O Lord, is the greatness, and the power, and the glory, and the victory, and the majesty. (1 Chronicles 29 : 11)

Enlarge Your Vision

THE telescope enlarges our vision upward. The microscope (or magnifying glass) enlarges our vision downward. Religion enlarges our vision inward. Christ enlarges our vision everywhere.

Christ never used the word " religion." He came to teach Life. And that word He used constantly. He came so that we " might have life and have it more abundantly."

Spiritual vision is the searchlight that guides us through life. Prayer wipes away the mist of our unknowing so we see face to face the perfection that God created and which He never mars.

Christ used the method of parable to teach the depth, breadth and height of Reality. To Him the maid was not dead, but only sleeping. To Him the sick were born to be whole, and the blind were ready for sight. He taught that the ugly, evil and distorted appearance of things is temporal and hence must pass away. When we see through the eyes of Christ, the imagination is heightened to its spiritual level of insight. And then, recognizing the divine perfection of God's Plan, we may help Him to transform what He will because of our belief.

The abundant life is the unfolding, growing life which never ceases to progress toward its divine potential.

Our heavenly Father, make us instruments to help to bring Thy Kingdom of Heaven in its full beauty, love and harmony, from invisibility into visibility, out of the hearts of men.

> And I saw a new heaven and a new earth : for the first heaven and the first earth were passed away ; and there was no more sea. And I John saw the holy city, new Jerusalem, coming down from God out of heaven, prepared as a bride adorned for her husband. (Revelation 21 : 1, 2)

Immerse " Self " in Living Waters

USE your imagination to witness the healing of Naaman in the Jordan. See him slowly wade out into the water, feel the coolness creeping higher and higher, healing the aching sores, cleaning and soothing all his flesh. Now he turns and walks toward the land again. Bright hot sunrays bathe his head and neck, shoulders and chest, until finally he emerges completely from the water and thus is completely submerged in sunlight.

Naaman was healed of leprosy through the miracle of water and sunlight. Years later John the Baptist lifted the process into a spiritual sacrament of " baptism by water and by fire."

Now think of yourself receiving this same baptism. Entering the waters, feel their cleansing and healing coolness cover you completely. Now turn, in imagination, and walk out into the sunlight. You are fresh, transparent, incandescent—sinless as the day you were born! Know that you are beautiful, perfect—reflecting the Light of God in your body, mind and soul. Incandescent, divine light illumines your face and form, revealing the rising sun of righteousness. So, emerge, Body Electric! Arise, shine! Your light has come! The Body Electric is here! It is yours! Your body is an emanation of pure water and sun. Your glorious Being uncovers its beauty and splendour with such effulgence as mortal eyes cannot behold. For you show forth the glorious beams of God's transcendent Love, melting infection and illness as dew before the sun.

When Jesus stepped into this realization on Mt. Hermon His garments shone as a fuller's cloth and even His disciples could not see Him for the Light.

Our Father, as the drop of water yields itself to the sun, teach us now to yield to the drawing power of The Son of Righteousness that we, like drops of water, may be drawn upward, perfected and translated in the higher realms of glory. On earth may we reflect the Light of Heaven, in Jesus' name. Amen.

Be ye therefore perfect, even as your Father which is in heaven is perfect.
(Matthew 5 : 48)

Unfailing Warmth of God's Love

I LOOK out upon the clean white snow. Inside my home I am warm and
comfortable. Oil heats each room, and I do not even need to go down
to tend the furnace any more. For twenty-five years I shovelled coal
and dumped the ashes ; now this home automatically heats itself. Now a
thermostat takes care of the adjustments which keep our temperature constant. And all because I substituted a fluid, floating form of heating material
for the solid chunks of coal.

Were these automatic servants available twenty-five years ago ? Oh, yes,
and long before that. Oil has been cached for millenniums in recesses
beneath the soil. The method of discovery, withdrawal and refinement
has been inherent in the intelligence, co-ordination and correlation of
human mind, muscle and nerve. It was waiting for us to use all this time.
Resting back now in my armchair by this window I see a beautiful white
world. I know it is cold outside, and I know that pain and sorrow and
ugliness are there. But forces are available to meet every human need,
when man is AWARE of them.

My thermostat was invented because someone was sensitive to the needs
of man and had faith in the resources of God.

O, Father in heaven, let *me* be one of your thermostats! I long to direct
the flow of that MIGHTIEST FORCE IN THE UNIVERSE—prayer! I long to
draw, by faith, from the abundance of Your storehouse, that the Kingdom
may come upon earth as it is in heaven.

> Because he hath set his love upon me, therefore will I deliver him : I will
> set him on high, because he hath known my name. He shall call upon me,
> and I will answer him : I will be with him in trouble ; I will deliver him,
> and honour him. With long life will I satisfy him, and show him my
> salvation. (Psalm 91 : 14–16)

Trust Completely

Your hopes for men should be great and dynamic, not little wishy-washy, insipid half-glimmers of optimism. Your love for men should be outgoing tidal waves that are clean and pure, and not little personal attachments, from which you withdraw when they take a false step. And your faith in your heavenly Father must be so complete that it *will* move mountains.

Look upward toward God as One whose Love is as infinite as the sky is infinite and whose Power compels all, even to the farthest ends of the universe. Now pray to Him, and—like a parachutist—jump off, right where you are now, into the surrounding atmosphere. Trust that the parachute is going to open, and that you are already safe. Now if air can support a parachute, how much more sufficient is the Love of God to support your prayer!

The most difficult law to obey in the kindergarten of prayer is this law of trusting relinquishment. To give a desire, or a dream, or your loved one, or yourself WHOLLY into God's care means not only that you trust God, but that you trust His Power. Then, letting God use time in His way, and every avenue and agency which He chooses, you wait calmly while he brings answers to your prayers down into the realm of tangible realities.

O Father, our hearts are Thine; all that we have is Thine. Take us, lead us, use us wherever Thou wilt. We have no fear, for we know Thy universe is filled with beauty, joy and love because it is Thine. Father, Thou hast given us our hopes and dreams. We trust Thee to unfold them in time to save us from despair. Indeed we have no disappointment even now, for we are falling into the arms of a perfect, Loving Master. Amen.

For he shall give his angels charge over thee. . . . They shall bear thee up in their hands. (Psalm 91 : 11-12)

Power in Love and Joy

THE inevitable result of every loving action is Joy.
The inevitable result of every joyous action is Power ;
The inevitable result of every powerful action is Glory.

For man rejoices in beholding the glory of God's perfect expression.
For man knows there is no material action, that all action is spiritual.
And the expression or objectification of this spiritual activity gives man
infinite joy and infinite happiness.
For man is the true perception of the true activity which is Love,
And he rejoices in the beauty of God's perfect spiritual activity.

Man does not have concern for himself, for Love is the only Motive Power.
And Love circulates all of God's ideas in perfect combinations, in perfect
regularity and in perfect sequence.

All are one in the body of Christ Jesus ;
Every member in particular is God's, and performs in His image and likeness.
Now, this moment, man reflects every capacity of God in all its power and
all its glory, in all its wholeness and all its perfection.

Man does not express himself, but rejoices in witnessing the joyous ex-
pression of God through him, and through others.
He realizes the infinite unity of the body of Christ,
For he is the unresisting witness of God's imperishable glory.

Nothing can prevent man from expressing the power and glory of God.
Nothing can prevent man from rejoicing at the power and glory of God
as expressed in others ;
Nothing can prevent man from seeing all God's perfect and joyous ideas
mingling in beautiful and harmonious combinations.

For Love is the power that circulates all God's ideas,
And Love is omnipotent, for Love is God.

> For I am persuaded, that neither death, nor life, nor angels, nor princi-
> palities, nor powers, nor things present, nor things to come, nor height, nor
> depth, nor any other creature, shall be able to separate us from the love
> of God, which is in Christ Jesus our Lord. (Romans 8 : 38, 39)

My Peace I Give Unto You

QUIETNESS and stillness always come *first* in everything that has permanence to it. Jesus' thirty " silent years " came before His three years of active ministry. In the Shepherd Psalm " He maketh me to *lie down* in green pastures " comes before " He *leadeth me* beside the still waters." In the phrase, " In quietness and confidence shall be my strength," it is noteworthy that *quietness* goes before *confidence.*

Not only does quietness come first in time, but it comes first in degree, in value. " Martha, Martha, thou art careful and troubled about many things. But one thing is needful ; and Mary hath chosen the better part, which shall not be taken away from her."

Not only is quietness and silence first in time and in value, it actually surrounds, covers, fills, all the rest. Quietness, if properly done, is ALL. A seed if it lets itself fall into the ground and is properly still does not have to do anything else . . . all is done. A sitting hen, if properly quiet, needs do nothing else. The same with us. If we are properly still, God does all the rest.

When you feel anxiety fading like a summer cloud, you may know that your prayer is being answered. When you pray with a group, and experience a deep peace in their presence, that is God's assurance that your prayer is to be answered. If peace becomes a sense of joy or ecstasy, a miracle is taking place at that moment in the mind and body of the one for whom you pray. This is the peace that passes understanding.

For God is our Father ; to accept any other idea of God will defeat any prayer before it is uttered. He is Love and therefore we may come to Him with perfect trust like good children. Oh that the globe were encircled completely with loving groups of praying persons, who invite the presence of God through Christ every day of every week in the Year!

If a man love me, he will keep my words : and my Father will love him, and we will come unto him, and make our abode with him. (John 14: 23)

Valleys of the Kingdom

You and I must be valleys—like the lovely valleys we are passing through now. There they lie at the foot of the giant mountains. Valleys are not curious, are not puffed up, are not climbing constantly to peep over to see how things are turning out in the great beyond. They do not stand apart, as mountains, in lonely glory. Valleys attend to their own humble business of carrying God's living waters down to the lowlands. They do not concern themselves with results. They know their only importance is in their willingness to be channels.

We want to be channels—deep and unobstructed—through which God's torrential Love may flow.

Father, we would bring healing to the souls of men. And through their souls, to the bodies and minds of men. And through the souls and minds and bodies to the governments of men. Heal the nations, O Lord! May our souls' sincere desires for the saving of Thy world be the very heartbeats of Almighty Love.

Thou art the Valley and the Mountain, the Water and the Cloud! Thou art Majestic and Eternal—the Beginning and the End. Thou art one God.

> He sendeth forth springs into the valleys :
> They run among the mountains ;
> They give drink to every beast of the field ;
> The wild animals quench their thirst.
> By them the birds of the heavens have their habitation ;
> They sing among the branches.
> He watereth the mountains from his chambers :
> The earth is filled with the fruit of thy works.
> He causeth the grass to grow for the cattle,
> And herb for the service of man ;
> That he may bring forth food out of the earth,
> And wine that maketh glad the heart of man,
> And oil to make his face to shine,
> And bread that strengtheneth man's heart.

> Psalm 104 : 10-15, A.S.V.

How to Become an Irresistible Person

SINCE God has arranged all things in this universe, and has appointed the time for the rising and the setting of the sun, and for the ebb and flow of the tides, He has also appointed the time that you should be in this world. He has selected the parents and duties that shall be yours. Whatever your present capacities or present opportunities for service, God's Plan for you is far more important than you now realize. His Plan for your life is to be a healthy, happy expression for the good of all. And so any work in which you have a natural sense of harmony with others, and which gives you joy, is yours to do now.

The essential purpose of life is to keep in touch with the Father and allow the Divinity that is in you to manifest. When a man or woman is attuned to God's will he is irresistible, no matter what duties he performs. Never did the world so need men and women with this cosmic sense of destiny. Never did God so need irresistible persons!

Since God has appointed the time for your influence to be spent here, let it be a time and an influence that builds for the Kingdom!

Our Father, we do not pray for easy lives ; we pray to be stronger men. We do not pray for tasks equal to our powers ; we pray for powers equal to our tasks. Turn our disappointments into Thy appointments.

> My son, forget not my law ; but let thine heart keep my commandments : for length of days, and long life, and peace, shall they add to thee. Let not mercy and truth forsake thee : bind them about thy neck ; write them upon the table of thine heart. So shalt thou find favour and good understanding in the sight of God and man. Trust in the Lord with all thine heart ; and lean not unto thine own understanding. In all thy ways acknowledge him, and he shall direct thy paths. (Proverbs 3 : 1–6)

Opening the Door to God

PRAYER is not a striving and a seeking, so much as it is a trustful opening of the doors of our spirits to let God enter, as the heart of a flower receives the sunlight when the petals unfold from the bud. Prayer is a listening, and a deepening of the consciousness that God is present when we call. Nay, " before we call Him He will answer."

It is helpful to begin the listening period with concentration on a simple promise of scripture. This is like taking a lantern and holding it in front of us to light our way. Sometimes God comes to us as inner vision on the canvas of the imagination, and we see realities beyond sensory perception. Sometimes He comes as a Voice speaking to the heart, or just as music upon the soul. The shepherds, watching their flocks by night, did not see the star; they heard the angel choirs. The wise men did not hear the music; they saw the star.

And so we do not strain to move from thought to thought in verbal prayer, but quietly and confidently we dwell upon some sentence from the Bible or other inspirational reading which helps us to realize anew the Loving-kindness of God, His all-pervading power, His willingness to impart peace and joy to the soul.

When others need our prayers we simply wait until the lamp we hold has driven back the shadows of our doubt and fear, and we see no evil. Then, recognizing the need of the sufferer, with perfect faith in God's power to transform pain into release and joy, we let Him do His perfect work.

When we remain in the awareness of the Presence of God we need not strive for any results. For we know that He has a perfect plan, and that in His time and way our prayers will be answered. We do not make vain efforts, we do not suffer in our concern, when we rely on the strength of Christ and not upon our own. Then when God directs us to take action or give guidance, it will be a natural and pleasurable expression, growing out of sincere Love.

Be still, and know that I am God. (Psalm 46 : 10)

Whenever we try to tell our friends in what we think is plain, simple language that a very beautiful and helpful spiritual experience has come to us, we are probably trying to explain something which they have no precedent for understanding. Each time we tell our secret to another person we drain off some of its power. Friends and enemies alike may think we are " showing off "—indeed sometimes we are!

One of the hardest of crosses to bear, when dealing with sacred matters, is the simple admonition to " keep our mouths shut." When one has such an experience it is an adventure in a new land, involving the use of a new language if we are to go very far. The words we use to explain it may be the same words we used before, but now they take on an entirely new meaning for us.

Jesus told us to erase our Selves so completely out of the picture, through secrecy and anonymity, that our right hand shall not see what the left hand is doing. If, in longing to share our great blessing, we desire to bring a blessing of renewed faith to another, there is one way only to achieve this. Let the still small voice of God speak within our hearts the words of guidance which will give us the authority to tell whatever will be most helpful. Resting in this inner stillness, in the centre of His power, we discover all truths drawn into perfectly adjusted and harmonious relationships. Divested of Self, we become like conches, which echo the music of the ocean's flow and tell secrets of Love to the listening ear.

Therefore when thou doest thine alms, do not sound a trumpet before thee. (Matthew 6 : 2)

The Drawing Power of God

THE sun's rays purge, cleanse and purify the things of this world. But the Light of God's Love is the most purging and purifying power available to man. By exposing oneself to this marvellous Light, in periods of complete silence, stillness and surrender, we receive the highest blessing.

Through such experiences, faithfully accepted day after day, we are cleansed of every residue of false thinking and consequent evil-doing. For the average person it is best to begin the Quiet Time with a period of complete relaxation and stillness. It is wonderful to sit for five minutes, ten or even fifteen, without tensing a single muscle or straining to receive insight. But this experience, seemingly so simple to achieve, is actually a most difficult discipline. Except in Quaker groups, certain Catholic monastic orders and some Hindu cults, the full power and blessing of silence is rarely understood.

Jesus set the example for us by going out regularly in the early dawn to expose Himself anew to the Love and Guidance of Almighty God. By this process He gained His power to transform lives. Surely we cannot be more independent than Christ, from the Source of Life!

O Man of Galilee, take us into the Garden with You, and there let us leave our selfish desires and dreams. Show us the secret places of the most high, that we too may " abide in the shadow of the Almighty."

> The earth is full of the lovingkindness of the Lord.
> By the word of the Lord were the heavens made,
> And all the host of them by the breath of his mouth.
> He gathereth the waters of the sea together as a heap :
> He layeth up the deeps in storehouses.
> Let all the inhabitants of the world stand in awe of him.
> For he spake, and it was done ;
> He commanded, and it stood fast. . . .
> The counsel of the Lord standeth fast for ever,
> The thoughts of his heart to all generations.
>
> (Psalm 33 : 5-11, A.S.V.)

And now, O Father, glorify thou me with thine own self with the glory which I had with thee before the world was. (John 17 : 5)

When You and Your Prayer Become One

LASH on flash of truth burst upon him. As the lightning lightens the heavens, even so the Truth illumined his soul, until he knew no barrier of flesh or of time or of circumstance between himself and the truth as he beheld it. For he was carried on an odyssey of the soul impossible to describe. As he seemed to rise it was not Space that flitted past him, but living things and all—all were growing with the speed of light, bursting from bloom to ripened fruit, the fruit in turn bearing more seeds which scattered again into new fulfilment. The vastness and the increase could not be measured. All around were heavenly colours, lights, fragrance and sound. Truth was not perceived by him, was not comprehended or caught, or wished for, or seen through a glass darkly. He had become, for the first time, the full instrument of Truth.

Then, gently, he returned to earthly consciousness, hearing the familiar purr of his clock on the mantel shelf. The hands pointed to almost the same time they recorded when he last looked. The study was still and he was alone. Suddenly he prayed, " O splendour of God, while I yet behold that consummate triumph of truth, grant me the memory of this moment forever, for this moment is the only real time in eternity! "

He did not speak or really think those words ; he *was* that prayer. And in his heart—now glowing like a flame—he had but one desire : to express in deed and thought that flash of divine revelation to the glory of God for the rest of his days.

> O God, thou art my God : Earnestly will I seek thee : My soul thirsteth for thee, my flesh longeth for thee, in a dry and weary land, where no water is. So have I looked upon thee in the sanctuary, to see thy power and thy glory. Because thy lovingkindness is better than life, my lips shall praise thee. So will I bless thee while I live : I will lift up my hands in thy name. My soul shall be satisfied as with marrow and fatness ; and my mouth shall praise thee with joyful lips ; when I remember thee upon my bed, and meditate on thee in the night-watches. For thou hast been my help and in the shadow of thy wings will I rejoice. (Psalm 63 : 1–7, A.S.V.)

Where Two or Three Agree Together

WHERE two or three gather together in His name, a magnet is created which draws down answers from heaven. If one prong of a magnet is broken off from the other, both prongs soon lose their drawing power. So one person separated from his fellow men can draw answers to prayer for awhile, but eventually he will lose all power in prayer unless he is reunited in spirit with others. And why? Because he cannot be magnetized with Love unless he knows love through human channels.

When two persons come together and " agree as to what they shall ask " their unity unlocks the doors of love in their hearts. This is like unlocking the power of gravity—whose spiritual counterpart draws upward to God those sincere prayers which only God can answer. " And I, if I be lifted up, will draw all men unto me," Christ promised.

AND WHATSOEVER YE SHALL ASK IN MY NAME, THAT WILL I DO, THAT THE FATHER MAY BE GLORIFIED IN THE SON. IF YE SHALL ASK ANY THING IN MY NAME, I WILL DO IT. (John 14 : 13–14.) Jesus was talking to His disciples when He made this promise. He knew their love for each other and for Him was great enough to ensure their prayers would be answered. For God's power cannot be misused, exploited or denied. What we ask in Christ's name we ask in His spirit.

> I am the vine, you are the branches. He who abides in me, and I in him, he it is that bears much fruit, for apart from me you can do nothing. If a man does not abide in me, he is cast forth as a branch and withers ; and the branches are gathered, thrown into the fire and burned. If you abide in me, and my words abide in you, ask whatever you will, and it shall be done for you. By this my Father is glorified, that you bear much fruit, and so prove to be my disciples. As the Father has loved me, so have I loved you ; abide in my love. If you keep my commandments, you will abide in my love, just as I have kept my Father's commandments and abide in his love. These things I have spoken to you, that my joy may be in you, and that your joy may be full. This is my commandment, that you love one another as I have loved you. . . . You did not choose me, but I chose you and appointed you that you should go and bear fruit and that your fruit should abide ; so that whatever you ask the Father in my name, he may give it to you. This I command you, to love one another. (John 15 : 5–12, 16–17, R.S.V.)

The Great Discovery

WE are told that the only way to find God is through meditation and prayer. But there is a greater discovery which, when truly understood, makes you master over *all* circumstances. And it is this: GOD IS EVERYWHERE. That means He is in the " without " just as surely as He is in the "within."

Since I have come to a truer understanding of this revelation I give much more of my time to putting in order the apparent disorders of outer circumstances. This does not mean that I give less time to prayer; it means that I pray so as to gain spiritual insight, to see through outer appearances of evil and discord into the Heart of Things. Jesus spoke " as one having authority and not as the scribes " because He gave precedence to the essential order of the universe and thereby gave it authority to manifest, in the name of our Maker. Jesus spoke with perfect Truth because He saw to the core, or Reality, in every situation, and Reality is perfect, immutable and creative.

One does not have to read all the daily newspapers in order to find the " news of the week "; he may see it condensed in a newsreel theatre or read it on a few pages of a weekly magazine. And it is not only in daily meditation and prayer that one discovers God's unfolding Plan; the " prayer of the week " is cast upon the vital events unfolding continually about us.

So, FIND GOD IN THE ROUTINE OF LIFE. Greet each new day with expectancy and wonder, like a little child. Move courageously into the main streams of life, appreciate all the earnest efforts of other persons, lend them your support to establish God's purposes, and believe in the *real love* which motivates even their crudest attempts to give aid and comfort. See every other human being as a divine instrument and *accept all of the events of your life* with the radiant certainty that God is in them!

> If I ascend up into heaven, thou art there : if I make my bed in hell, behold, thou art there. If I take the wings of the morning, and dwell in the uttermost parts of the sea; even there shall thy hand lead me. (Psalm 139 : 8–10)

There Is a Rightful Place for Everyone

Have you found your right place in life?

Are you lonely, frustrated or confused?

Then enter the Secret Place of the Most High and absorb and be absorbed by the Infinite Love of God. Forgive your enemies, take those who are near and dear to you deeply into your heart, and become very still. Then listen to the still small Voice.

There is a perfect law of supply and demand, the Voice will tell you. When a man is completely surrendered to God, if he needs anything, he knows exactly where to get it. When he wishes to pass on an idea he knows exactly where to pass it. Love is the power that brings these ideas into perfectly harmonious activity, and Love is omnipotent, for Love is God.

There is not a negative-poled atom in the universe unless there is a positive-poled atom somewhere to match it. There is no one with capacity to serve unless there is somewhere a need for that service; and when one yields himself utterly to the Love of God the need and supply will find each other out. Love is the perfect medium of exchange, for Love is the power that brings all God's ideas into perfectly adjusted and harmonious activity.

There is no separation; there is only one Mind—God, and one consciousness—man. Therefore man is instantly in touch with any person he needs, for all are one body in Christ. Each member is God's image and likeness, and we together realize the perfect unity of the body of Christ.

> There is one body, and one Spirit, even as ye are called in one hope of your calling; one Lord, one faith, one baptism, one God and Father of all, who is above all, and through all, and in you all. But unto every one of us is given grace according to the measure of the gift of Christ. . . . That we henceforth be no more children, tossed to and fro, and carried about with every wind of doctrine, by the sleight of men, and cunning craftiness, whereby they lie in wait to deceive; but speaking the truth in love, may grow up into him in all things, which is the head, even Christ. (Ephesians 4: 4–7, 14–15)

Each Day a New Adventure

THE simplest and surest way to rid ourselves of sin, sickness or other betraying evils is to melt our Selves down—as an old coin is melted at the mint—and be re-created, fresh and new. We may do this by turning and becoming as nearly as possible like little children. A gnarled old tree bears brand-new leaves each spring that are as fresh and new as the original sprout which pushed through the ground. Why don't we investigate and discover whether we too may possess within ourselves somewhere a fountain of ever-renewing life?

If our bodies seem too " solid " to change immediately into healthy new embodiments for our souls, let us see what we can do with our imaginations. Let us try to think like children—full of daydreams, looking at life with continual expectancy and an ever-renewed sense of wonder. Children expect each day will provide a new adventure.

But old persons' thoughts get into frames. Of course anything which is held tight in a frame is brittle and can be broken. Therefore the " frames " of bad habits, prejudices and meaningless traditions should be cast off to allow pure, flowing, vital new ideas to flow through our souls.

Learn new hobbies, read new books, travel to strange new places. Ask God to give you beautiful dreams and greater visions. And above all EXPECT LIFE TO BE BEAUTIFUL. With eyes of childlike trust and love, look toward your Father, God, as toward a perfect, ideal and devoted Parent.

My son, keep my words, and lay up my commandments with thee. Keep my commandments, and live ; and my law as the apple of thine eye. Bind them upon thy fingers, write them upon the table of thine heart. Say unto wisdom, thou art my sister ; and call understanding thy kinswoman. (Proverbs 7 : 1–4)

Whosoever shall not receive the kingdom of God as a little child, he shall not enter therein. (Mark 10 : 15)

Forgiveness of Christ

THE only way to receive perfect cleansing from sin and sickness is through repentance. The publican in the temple who said, " God be merciful to me a sinner," received the blessing of Christ's promised redemption. Whenever a prodigal returns saying, " I have sinned against heaven and in thy sight," we know he is coming Home to the Love of an all-forgiving heavenly Father.

One of the most difficult blessings to accept, however, is this cleansing through the Forgiveness of Christ. Many persons who suffer physical sickness remain uncured simply because they cannot believe in the healing power of repentance. And so we must try to recognize this purging, drawing power of God's Love, so that we can yield ourselves trustingly to Him for complete cleansing.

Suppose we think of it this way: God has celestial vacuum cleaners which His angels can use to draw out all poisons, toxins and infections in our souls and bodies. So let us invite the Lord to send down a corps of Angel Cleaners, and put them to work right now. As they are invisible, they can penetrate into any pocket or hidden area of our lives, and turn on their celestial vacuums. Since these angels neither slumber nor sleep, let them keep on the job all day and all night—for a week, if necessary, or a month. Let them go clear through the corridors of time, even into our babyhood, and open hidden closets which may conceal that terrible fright in infancy, those frustrations of youth and resentments of middle age.

Pray to the Father that they will not work too fast, as you do not want them to cause any pain. And then tell Him you are waiting for His healing Love to flow in, until the heavenly transfusions of the blood of Christ heal all the sores and fill all the empty places. Thank Him now, in Jesus' Name, and rise up—a new creation!

> Purge me with hyssop, and I shall be clean : wash me, and I shall be whiter than snow. Make me to hear joy and gladness ; that the bones which thou hast broken may rejoice. Hide thy face from my sins, and blot out all mine iniquities. Create in me a clean heart, O God ; and renew a right spirit within me. (Psalm 51 : 7–10)

In Rhythm with the Universe

THE easiest, most effortless motion is falling. And yet it is the most powerful. In fact the only perpetual motion one can conceive of— which would be in any sense practical—is the motion of the waterfall, whose water is continually drawn up from the earth by the sun and continually falls back to the rocks and streams. . . . All of the machinery of the world is in some way propelled by this rising and falling process of water which can be converted into steam or electricity and turns wheels. The movements of the stars in their courses, of the earth swinging in its orbit about the sun, and the moon about the earth—all are continually falling, falling, and always in their prescribed courses.

We in our little individual experiences find that the most propelling motions are essentially falling ones. But unfortunately these motions do not seem to be easy and continuous and automatic. We have to be primed, cranked, re-started, otherwise we soon " run down " or fall on our faces instead of our feet. But if we were perfectly attuned to God's laws, had man never fallen out of Eden, perhaps we should not have to be thus " catching ourselves " all the time. If we were as surrendered to the Light of God as the water is to the sun, we too could come up over every problem which confronts us.

Perhaps when we die and go to heaven we shall find there that we need only fall easily and naturally—but always into perfect alignment with God, into perfect relationships with others, into loves that are divinely reciprocated, falling, falling . . . into great big beautiful realms of consciousness where happiness and glory come from the Power to bless mankind. Could there be a happier conception of heaven ? Indeed I think the saint must be one who has so completely given himself to God that he need only keep falling forever, in rhythm with the universal Laws.

And I, if I be lifted up from the earth, will draw all men unto me. (John 12 : 32)

And if I go and prepare a place for you, I will come again. . . . (John 14 : 3)

72

... Of Strawberry Boxes and Vibrations

WHEN I was a small boy my brother and I loved to play with strawberry boxes, and after the strawberry season we were given the whole ones and the broken ones to do with as we wished. The whole boxes made castles, churches and houses. The broken ones we dismantled into strips, and these in turn we broke into various lengths to represent men, cannon, horses and cattle or even furniture and foodstuffs. We fought many a battle against the strawberry-stained Redskins!

I have since discovered that my brother and I were playing the " game " God plays all the time. And when we are attuned to Him, He can break up the vibrations of the universe into the lengths which we need. For instance, when we want stones and lumber for houses, He uses the very long wave lengths (a few vibrations per second), when we want water or wine, He breaks them smaller. Music comes in still shorter " strips," light and electricity are virtually pulverized, and magnetism and gravity—forces that hold the universe together—are composed of the most infinitesimal wave lengths.

Scientists say that a single spoonful of water contains enough energy to move our largest steamships across the ocean and back—if we could break up its vibrations sufficiently. We already know that a piece of uranium, shattered into atoms, will blast a city to ruin.

Yes, it all goes back to the strawberry boxes and vibrations. Give a small boy some strawberry boxes and a creative imagination, and he will build a " world." Give God the love of a son, and He can break it up into the most powerful force in the universe, transforming the son himself into a new creature and the world in which he lives into a new creation.

Behold, I will make thee a new sharp threshing instrument having teeth : thou shalt thresh the mountains, and beat them small, and shalt make the hills as chaff. Thou shalt fan them, and the wind shall carry them away, and the whirlwind shall scatter them : and thou shalt rejoice in the Lord, and shalt glory in the Holy One of Israel. (Isaiah 41 : 15–16)

And God Saw That It Was Good

LIGHT is the source of all life. The earth was created from the sun, as though projected from its womb, and ever since has turned back toward the source of its creation like a child seeking to derive its sustenance from its mother's breast. And all that grows upon the earth looks toward the sun for life.

The lily of the field is blessed with some primary inner alchemy which converts the light of the sun directly into its life. But the cow and sheep have not this same primary alchemy, and so they turn to the lily, and to other growing plants of the field, for their sustenance. The sun which filters through the porous blades of the grasses enters the flesh and blood of flocks which graze in the fields.

Man, still further removed from the elementary alchemy of nature, cannot be satisfied with eating grass and other products of the field, so he turns to cattle and sheep—beef and mutton—and thus takes the sustenance of the sun thirdhand for his consumption.

All things, insofar as they wish to live, find themselves dependent upon the sun.

Now prayer in its simplest form is just looking up toward the Son of God as the Source of Light and Life. Unfortunately we often build sheds of resentment or fear or indifference over our heads, and live in shadow much of our lives. And yet if we could step out directly under the Son, and yield ourselves like the lily to His Light, we should be as care-free and content as children in homes of happiness.

> Consider the lilies of the field, how they grow : they toil not, neither do they spin : And yet I say unto you, that even Solomon in all his glory was not arrayed like one of these. Wherefore, if God so clothe the grass of the field, which to-day is, and to-morrow is cast into the oven, shall he not much more clothe you, O ye of little faith ? Therefore take no thought, saying, What shall we eat ? or, What shall we drink ? or, Wherewithal shall we be clothed ? ... For your heavenly Father knoweth that ye have need of all these things. (Matthew 6 : 28–32)

Because They Loved Me

Who made me ?
Those who love me!
God, first, because He loves me the most ;
My parents next, because they loved me next—
And their love brought me into being.

But when I was " born " was I created ?
Not wholly ; my creation had just begun.
For I am created anew every day, every hour that I live,
Since each one who loves me re-creates me in his heart.
Yes, he carries me in the womb of his thoughts, in his love—my
embryo soul—
And sends me forth anew with every breath he breathes.

As long as I have friends to love me, the process of my creation continues
As friends increase and as their love for me deepens
I can express that Love outward, in ever-widening circles.
For as Love is infinite, so is its expression.
And each day that confronts me brings more glorious, inexpressible
rapture!

And how much have all my efforts achieved ?
Nothing!
They are not mine at all, but yours—you who created me.

And this, out of a heart of gratitude, shall be my prayer :
That I in my day may create many reborn souls with you who love me.
You and God and I, breathing our prayers together,
Will bring them to rebirth.
It will be our secret partnership with God—
The three of us in One—and you and I are part of Creation,
Linked with the spheres . . . by that Love which is
In Jesus Christ.

And God said, Let us make man in our image, after our likeness ; and let
him have dominion . . . over all the earth. (Genesis 1 : 26)

Power in Stillness

THE material world is a sort of mirrored semblance of the spiritual world. But from a material point of view everything in it is exactly the reverse of what it would be from a spiritual point of view.

Stillness in the physical or material realm, for instance, spells lethargy. Stillness in the spiritual or heavenly realm spells ecstasy. The silence of the dunce and the silence of the saint are not the same silences.

Motion in the physical realm involves varying degrees of friction. The old trap travelling seven miles an hour over a bumpy country road has more jerk and bounce than a modern car travelling sixty miles an hour on cushion tyres. A train running on carefully laid tracks has still less friction in contact with the ground, and an airplane rising above the earth attains the smoothest motion of all. But in the spiritual realm no friction exists, and the stiller we are, the faster we are actually moving.

Thus, the world would be far more creative and far less wasteful if every man, woman and child spent more time in meditation and prayer, and less time in so-called active, productive efforts. For in the very Centre of the greatest motion of all, which is Love, all desires are fulfilled, everything is accomplished at the right time, every word spoken is the right word, and two or three hours of work a day would be sufficient to bring together the producer and the consumer, the writer and the reader, the speaker and the audience. And the " wise and prudent " would then indeed be amazed at the wealth and peace and joy which the world contains.

Be still, and know that I am God. (Psalm 46 : 10)

The Divine Counsellor

ERHAPS with the analogy of the stereoscope we can understand better the secret process by which the Kingdom comes into manifestation on Earth. Christ explained it perfectly in the Sermon on the Mount, and yet we often have difficulty in comprehending His full meaning.

In the stereoscope there are two miniature panes of optical glass through which one looks, not at just one picture, but at two pictures of the same scene. Yet the two are not taken from exactly the same point of view. One is taken a few paces to the right of the other. The two pictures are similar in that they represent the same scene, and yet dissimilar in that they are taken from separated standpoints. But in each case two images merge giving the effect of one. And when your eyes get into focus (or as Jesus put it, " when your eye is single ") you find that you are no longer looking at a flat view, but as it were through a doorway into a new world with heights and depths and shadows. Indeed you may be tempted to step through the doorway and stroll down the country lane or city street that opens before you. In other words, a couple of two-dimensional pictures brought into focus under the principle of dynamic symmetry, open for you a three-dimensional world.

Now when two persons, a teacher and pupil, come together, and are in tune with each other, seeking a common goal in love and trust and joy, new vistas of the true, the beautiful and the good open continually before them.

Let Christ be your teacher and learn of Him through His words. Because you cannot stand just where He stood, you will take your picture from a little different point of view. But because you are looking together, you will discover the Realities of Heaven right here on earth.

> And it shall come to pass afterward, that I will pour out my spirit upon all flesh ; and your sons and your daughters shall prophesy, your old men shall dream dreams, your young men shall see visions. . . . And I will shew wonders in the heavens and in the earth. (Joel 2 : 28, 30)

Whatsoever You Ask in My Name

J ESUS said that anything, any miracle, could be accomplished if asked
in His NAME. To Jesus the Name or the Word signified the entire
being—the whole idea, the perfect totality. Each individual should
be considered as a *whole* individual, and not as a fragmentary one. In short,
he should be considered as a man and not as a publican or sinner or fisher-
man or husbandman. And when a person is totally united with God he
becomes as it were the entire universe conscious at one point. Christ told
people they could become sons of God. And when He told them this He
gave them a new awareness, a sense of unity with God and each other,
which when fully comprehended is called the " kingdom consciousness."

But unfortunately no-one except the Master Himself achieved a complete
realization of His sonship. Indeed there was begotten in Him from birth
this consciousness of oneness with the Father. A philosopher might say
that Jesus was " the universe conscious at one point." For with such a
realization He became a channel through which all the power of the universe
could flow.

And so Jesus promised continually that anything we could ask for with
His consciousness, would be granted us.

Verily, verily, I say unto you, Whatsoever ye shall ask the Father in
my name, he will give it you. Hitherto have ye asked nothing in my
name: ask, and ye shall receive, that your joy may be full. (John 16:
23–24)

O Lift Up Your Heads

THERE are three levels of truth: the sky level, the street level and the sewer level. If you want " the facts of life " you must admit that all are there. But we can choose what facts we want to dwell upon, and what level of truth we want to live with. I for one do not choose to live in the sewer.

" But that is escape," the cynic shouts. " You are running from reality."

Of course it is escape. Who would not escape from the sewer level as fast as he could? Let the researchers do their investigating there; let the plumbers mend the pipes there; but unless your business requires your presence, leave that level of truth to those whose duty is there.

But up on the street level where you belong, plant your feet firmly and get the work done which God gave you to do—as accurately, thoroughly and effectively as possible. Only do not think that that is the only level where truth can be found!

Spend a part of each day on the sky level. In the early dawn before the work of the day begins, pause and look with eyes of wonder into the sky, and listen with Job to the Voice of the Lord saying: " Where wast thou when I laid the foundations of earth? . . . Or who laid the cornerstone thereof, when the morning stars sang together and all the sons of God shouted for joy? . . . Who can number the clouds in wisdom? "

O Lord, my God, open my eyes that I may see visions of Truth Thou hast for me!

For where your treasure is, there will your heart be also. (Matthew 6: 21)

Let God do the Creating

WE are on the verge of a great discovery, the discovery that GREAT RICHES, LOVELY IDEAS, AND MASTERPIECES ARE ALREADY CREATED IN THE MIND OF GOD.

> There is an inmost centre in us all,
> Where truth abides in fulness ; and around,
> Wall upon wall, the gross flesh hems it in,
> This perfect, clear perception—which is truth.
> A baffling and perverting carnal mesh
> Binds it, and makes all error : and, to KNOW,
> Rather consists in opening out a way
> Whence the imprisoned splendour may escape,
> Than in effecting entry for a light
> Supposed to be without.
>
> ROBERT BROWNING

Nothing tires a creative person, or a scholar, so much as the feeling that he must do the creating and thinking himself. Vital currents of Truth are constantly flowing as perfect, pure inspiration. But to receive them we must be responsive first to the needs in the hearts of men and then think of our minds and imaginations as the vortex through which God may draw a response to meet those needs.

Work with ease and joy! And know that only God can give you true inspiration ; this relieves you from the tensions of effort and frustration. The greatest genius of all has said, " I do not do these works, but the Father in me doeth them." Does a miner claim to have created coal when he sinks his shaft into the earth to that point where God placed it millions of years ago ?

When Jesus went up into the mountain to pray, He left behind the limited carpenter consciousness and entered into Permanent Identity with God. We too can step out of our little Tom, Dick and Harry lives. A wire lying twisted in the alley is rubbish ; the same wire connected to a power-house can light every lamp in a city. Through prayer we make contact with the Powerhouse of God and become channels of blessing.

As the branch cannot bear fruit of itself, except it abide in the vine ;
no more can ye, except ye abide in me. (John 15 : 4)

I Am a Child of God

I AM a child, a child of Father-God,
And live forever in His Blessed Home.
The earth is His, the seas, the clod,
The very grass His rug, the sky His dome.

I meet sweet children, smiling as I pass,
And everywhere the Light of Love is bright
In flower and face and on the dew-pearl'd grass—
A heaven of sound and fragrance and of sight.

A child is yet a grown-up, though he's seen
As at a distance, and the grown-ups hear
His babble from afar because he's been
In the Kingdom Doorway now and here.

.   .   .   .   .   .

So though we scorn the babe and praise the man,
And though we change all innocence to art,
And use our Reason proudly as we can,
We'll find that children choose the better part.

Come join me on the playground God has planned.
We'll work for Him, but it will seem like play.
When I'm afraid I'll take my Father's hand
And trust His new-born world is on its way.

And whoso shall receive one such little child in my name receiveth me.
But whoso shall offend one of these little ones which believe in me, it
were better for him that a millstone were hanged about his neck, and
that he were drowned in the depth of the sea. . . . Take heed that ye
despise not one of these little ones; for I say unto you, that in heaven
their angels do always behold the face of my Father which is in heaven.
(Matthew 18: 5–6, 10)

God Has a Divine Plan for Me

I BELIEVE that the plan God has for me is wrapped in the folds of my being, even as the oak is wrapped in the acorn, and the rose in the bud. I believe that this Plan is permanent, indestructible and perfect—free from all that is essentially evil. Any negative experience has no part in my God-created Plan; it is simply a distortion caused by my own wilfulness and blindness. When I relax and yield trustingly to His leading, I lose all sense of personal responsibility for seeing that His will is done. And in that attitude of peaceful assurance His Plan works out perfectly for me and through me.

I may know when I am following His guidance, because only at those times do I have peace. And with it comes a creative urge, propelling me into joyous expression and activity; or it gives me patience and a willingness to sit back when others must unfold the Plan for me.

I believe that this Plan is a perfect part of the larger Plan for the good of all men, and that my good can never be separated from theirs. I believe I may accept with radiant acquiescence all the persons and events that come into my life, knowing that they have been sent to provide me with God-given opportunities for spiritual growth and service.

I believe that when I look out upon the world with trust and love I shall see the shining threads in the over-all Pattern which God has designed. And I shall discover that my own life is woven permanently into His eternal tapestries.

> And I heard a great voice out of heaven saying, Behold, the tabernacle of God is with men, and he will dwell with them, and they shall be his people, and God himself shall be with them, and be their God. And God shall wipe away all tears from their eyes; and there shall be no more death, neither sorrow, nor crying, neither shall there be any more pain: for the former things are passed away. (Revelation 21 : 3-4)

Seek Him With Your Whole Heart

WHAT does it mean to seek God with one's WHOLE heart? Did you ever have an experience in which you poured out every ounce of your energy, every atom of your desire, every resource of mind and soul and body—all at once?

At the age of twenty-two, in 1912, Clarence DeMar won the American Marathon. Ten years later he attempted to make a comeback, although other great winners had failed in the effort. As he ran that race he prayed with every fibre of his being, giving all his strength to the race and all his trust to God. Ten miles from the finish his strength began to give out and each step was anguish. Then suddenly a power from behind him seemed to push him on, his steps were lighter, and with comparative ease he ran through—a winner. Since then he has won other Marathons, and is the greatest American Marathoner of modern times.

Whether you are a mountain climber, singer, doctor, businessman or housewife, you may have experienced at some time the zest of doing something with all your heart. But one does not know the full joy of whole-hearted effort until he has experienced it in relation to other persons, and not as an independent achievement. When a man falls in love he suddenly comes into powers, courage and perseverance which he did not know he could possess. He goes about his tasks with a song on his lips, a psalm in his heart, and apparently moves upon wings. For once, he is seeking someone with his whole heart.

To-day let us fall in Love with God; let us seek Him morning, noon and night with all our heart, mind and soul, through Jesus Christ Our Lord.

Jesus said unto him, Thou shalt love the Lord thy God with all thy heart, and with all thy soul, and with all thy mind. This is the first and great commandment. And the second is like unto it, Thou shalt love thy neighbour as thyself. (Matthew 22 : 37–39)

From Under the Sheltering Wings

WHEN I was a boy raising chickens, I would place thirteen eggs under our hen and, twenty-one days later, about twelve of them would be transformed into lively, happy chirping chicks. I didn't have to do anything to help the hen; I just turned the whole job over to her. Since then it has come to me that we should be able to put at least as much trust in God as I put in that biddie-hen! And when we do, let me tell you what can happen.

Suppose you take a piece of paper and draw thirteen eggs. Write on each one the name of a person you want to pray for, or a problem you want to pray about. Then open your old family Bible to Psalm 91 and lay the entire " setting " of prayer-eggs between its pages. Place the Bible back upon the shelf, and mark on the calendar the date three weeks ahead when you can look for the hatched brood. But until that day do not peek for answers to your prayers! Just look forward expectantly and happily. And when the three weeks have passed take out the " shells " and see what they contained. Of course you may find one or two have not hatched. There are two reasons for failures in prayer-answers and egg-hatchings. If there is even a little rottenness—vanity, jealousy, greed, or desire to escape from reality—or if you pulled them out from the sheltering warmth of the Wings of the Almighty, in the Secret Place of the Most High, they will have missed some of the warm love they needed to come to birth.

But even those lively, downy little answers to your prayers will have to be gently nourished. They cannot crow and cackle and lay eggs the very first day! Place them now into the incubator of Luke 13, and let Jesus brood over the little fledglings in His loving way. Then see how they grow and spread their wings!

> O Jerusalem, Jerusalem . . . how often would I have gathered your children together as a hen gathers her brood under her wings, and you would not! (Luke 13 : 34, R.S.V.)

Prayer, the Mightiest Force

WHEN in all history has there been amassed so much knowledging as in the past fifty years? Through psychiatry nearly all the mysteries of the subconscious realm have been brought to light. And yet what have we learned about man's soul which was not brought to light by Christ? For years we have been flying through the air, and now with television we send pictures through space. For years we were harnessing waterfalls to turn great turbines, and now we harness the split atoms to fight battles for us. We are setting in motion forces which our forefathers could not even dream of! But how many of us have learned that the power of prayer is greater than the radio or television, and the power of love is greater than bombs?

Fifty years ago Steinmetz, electrical wizard and author of more than three hundred inventions, said: " For the past fifty years we have been working with the laws of matter. Fifty years from now we shall be making a study of the laws of spirit. When that time comes we shall take Love into the laboratory and find more power in Love than there is in electricity. When prayer is used with the same confidence that we now use the forces of matter, we shall achieve more in one generation than the world has achieved in the last four hundred years."

The fifty years are up now. Let us actually take Love and Prayer into the laboratory of the spirit and expect to witness miracles as great as the miracles of the radio and atomic bomb—and greater.

Our beloved Heavenly Father, may Thy Love flowing into us create in us a new love, a new understanding, a new life. May we step deep into the quiet of the Upper Room—the laboratory of Love—and there discover Thy precious Truths so that we may build for Thee Thy Kingdom according to the Plan and Purpose laid out in the beginning by Jesus Christ, Thy Son. Amen.

Thy kingdom come. Thy will be done in earth, as it is in heaven. (Matthew 6 : 10)

Dreams That Come True

As a youth Alexander the Great slept with a copy of Homer's story of Achilles beneath his pillow. Napoleon slept with a copy of the life of Alexander the Great under his pillow. Both these men looked into the timeless past for their inspiration; they visioned the years of future victory as already theirs. When Alexander set forth with a small army to conquer the world, an adviser said, " If you go forth to conquer, these men are too few; if to be conquered, they are too many." And to him Alexander replied, " You forget I have my hopes! "

If we follow the Lord with our whole heart, trust Him truly, have the courage to ask for difficult tasks and heroic accomplishments, it is because we have much HOPE. When Dante reached paradise with Beatrice he was told that others may have surpassed him in love and faith, but he surpassed them in hope. Yet hope is greatly neglected and little understood. There are two kinds of hope. There is the Mr. Micawber kind; he waited always for " something to turn up." And then there is the St. Paul kind. " In Christ is our hope," he said. The first is based on the weakness of wishful thinking. The second is based on the strength of God.

To gain Paul's kind of hope, it is helpful to try to step outside of the limits of space and time and think of ourselves as having been in some way present during all the moments of the past before Now and in all the moments of the future after Now. This view is like seeing a film, made up of thousands of " stills " rapidly passing in sequence before our eyes; it is very different from the view of a Micawber, who sits staring at one slide at a time, projected by an old-fashioned magic lantern!

I will praise thee;
For I am fearfully and wonderfully made:
Marvellous are thy works;
And that my soul knoweth right well.
My substance was not hid from thee,
When I was made in secret,
And curiously wrought in the lowest parts of the earth.
Thine eyes did see my substance, yet being unperfect;
And in thy book all my members were written,
Which in continuance were fashioned,
When as yet there was none of them.

(Psalm 139 : 14–16)

Seeking the Quiet Spaces

THE practice of Stillness is cumulative, like a snowball growing upon itself. It creates great Quiet Spaces in a man. " Do thou thyself but hold thy tongue for one day," writes Carlyle, " and on the morrow how much clearer are thy purposes, and duties ; what wreck and rubbish have the mute workmen within thee swept away when intrusive noises were shut out! "

To achieve Silence within means training in relaxation, in effortless motion, in selflessness, in complete self-effacement. There should be no seeking, no striving, no directed thinking whatever. There should be no striving even to see God. Rather, rest in the presence of God—yes, in His very bosom—and be cleansed of hypocrisy, anger, fear, jealousy, through the purifying, penetrating power of His Love. After ten, fifteen, even thirty minutes of purgation, we are ready to reach for, and take, all that is good, beautiful and true. Reach up to the heavens, reach for all that the heavens hold!

Every seed of life had its beginning in the place of Silence. The world of work and noise is all about us, despotic and uncompromising. Yet the world of Silence is all about us also. We can slip into it instantly, and when its mantle drops over our spirit we feel release, calmness and enlightenment. Silence will do this, but not reverie and vacant musings. It will be the Silence of the lone Figure of Gethsemane, girding Himself with equipment for every Victory.

I will lift up mine eyes unto the hills, from whence cometh my help. My help cometh from the Lord, which made heaven and earth. He will not suffer thy foot to be moved : he that keepeth thee will not slumber. Behold, he that keepeth Israel shall neither slumber nor sleep. The Lord is thy keeper : the Lord is thy shade upon thy right hand. The sun shall not smite thee by day, nor the moon by night. The Lord shall preserve thee from all evil : he shall preserve thy soul. The Lord shall preserve thy going out, and thy coming in, from this time forth, and even for evermore. (Psalm 121)

Riding On God's Train

LET us imagine that we are on a train which is carrying us to distant parts. Everything about the trip has been arranged according to law and order. When the time comes to eat, a waiter gives the call and dinner is served. When the time comes to sleep, a porter makes our seats into beds. The schedule is arranged so that we pass through beautiful scenery in the daytime and less interesting portions at night. We may even anticipate some of the excitement ahead, by reviewing the maps of the terrain.

But suppose now that we do not trust our Master Planner, who arranged the journey? We shall then lie awake half the night trying to peer behind a curtain of darkness at scenery which we think we should not miss. In consequence we shall be so drowsy during the daytime that we must nap when the train moves through beautiful countryside or past wonderful views. We may not even trust the sufficiency of the table d'hôte dinner promised for the evening, and begin to nibble biscuits and sweets during the afternoon, and thus be unable to eat the banquet when it is laid before us.

No matter how we try to rearrange the Plan it remains a perfectly ordered one. And others will find it so. Just because we happen to be asleep when the most magnificent scenes come into view does not mean they were never there. Just because we are unable to eat the dinner when it comes does not mean there was any insufficiency in the menu. Just because we cannot always read the road map does not mean it is inaccurate.

Why try to disarrange or avoid the Plan of God, or to supplant it with little insufficient, spiteful schemes of our own? Why not simply sit still and rest in peace and assurance while we move easily, smoothly, rhythmically onward according to the arrangements of the Master Planner?

Commit thy way unto the Lord; trust also in him; and he shall bring it to pass. (Psalm 37: 5)

Establish Ground Wires

ONCE upon a time a man attached a lightning rod to the chimney of his house and thought he would be safe from lightning in the skies. To his horror the house was struck during the next electric storm and burned to the ground. A stranger, hearing of this misfortune, advised the man: "Lightning is not confined to the skies; it is everywhere—in the ground under your feet and in the clouds over your head. So when you raise a lightning rod to the skies, sink another one into the earth, and you will be protected." The man heeded this advice and when he rebuilt his house it was safe.

Now many years later this same man fell ill with a disease for which his physician said there was no man-made cure. He advised his patient to seek God's healing aid. But the sick man had no faith in any kind of help that man could not administer and so he lay in bed and his condition grew constantly worse. At last he could scarcely move, and in desperation wrote to a stranger—a man of whom it had been said: "God works through his prayers." And he begged this man to pray for a cure. The stranger came to the bedside of the dying one, and took his hand. Then very kindly he spoke: "My friend, God's Love, expressed in healing power, is not limited to my little prayers, or my presence, or any particular creed or church. God, and all that He is, is available everywhere. He abides in you as He abides in me. You have been looking to others for help. Now sink your shafts of faith deep in your own heart. Establish ground wires to the Eternal Source of Life which may be tapped instantly with faith, to meet any real need."

The sick man remembered the advice of another stranger, and wondered at what he now heard. But he did obey, as before; he found that reservoir of Divine Power which is in the very ground beneath us as well as in the clouds overhead. Soon he was healed, and ever since he has longed to help others find their "ground wires."

Thy faith hath made thee whole. (Matthew 9:22)

Angels Shall Bear Thee Up

THERE is only one way to overcome fear and that is to keep in balance. Fears of physical injury are overcome when we learn how to move rhythmically and with easy co-ordination. Muscles at the back of the neck must be relaxed so that the head is kept in easy balance at the top of the spine. Skilled gymnasts and trained athletes are never afraid of falling because they know how to fall into balance.

Fears of the mind are overcome when the imagination is well-balanced. An arrested and inhibited imagination continually creates tensions by falsifying reality. When we can view life as a whole instead of in segments, when we can see beneath the appearance of evil to the divine progression toward fulfilment of needs, quietness and calmness are our portion. And then our ideas come to us in perfect order and perfect sequence.

Fears of the soul are overcome when the spirit is brought into balance. As tightened neck muscles unbalance our bodies, constricted love unbalances the spirit. When we can see all other persons as they really are —inherently perfect beings in a perfectly planned universe governed by a perfectly loving God—we have lost all fears. For Love is such a strong force that it needs no other forces to support or sustain it.

When we are balanced in body, mind and soul we are ready to " rise up on wings as eagles " to the heights of living where we truly belong. And then as we " fall " according to the pull of divine forces, we are safe and all our relationships are perfectly adjusted and harmonious.

He that overcometh shall inherit all things ; and I will be his God, and he shall be my son. (Revelation 21 : 7)

Let Us Share Our Brother's Burden

EVERY time you sit down to eat a meal without a thought, word or act of blessing for those who are without food, you are a partner in sin. Every day that you accept comfortable living without making protest or offering prayers against an economic order that begets tyrants, criminals and wars, you are a co-creator of those criminals and those wars. Every time you hold prejudice or contempt toward any race or class or nation, you are planting seeds of death and decay. Every time you harbour anger and resentment in your heart toward any living creature, you are pouring into the pure air about you poisons that create murderers. Every time you look with lust upon a woman you are adding to the danger that a less-controlled one may commit folly.

Therefore I say unto you, repent of the crimes in which you are an unconscious and unwitting partner. Take upon your shoulders the world's vast crime of indifference, inertia and selfish complacency, and kneel to repent for all. Jesus, who committed no sin or folly, will bless you for sharing the sins of the world and lifting them up to Him.

> If I have withheld the poor from their desire,
> Or have caused the eyes of the widow to fail;
> Or have eaten my morsel myself alone,
> And the fatherless hath not eaten thereof; . . .
> If I have seen any perish for want of clothing,
> Or any poor without covering; . . .
> And if he were not warmed with the fleece of my sheep;
> If I have lifted up my hand against the fatherless,
> When I saw my help in the gate :
> Then let mine arm fall from my shoulder blade,
> And mine arm be broken from the bone.
>
> (Job 31 : 16–22)

Everyone to His Place of Prayer!

I F I could find an Object worthy of my utmost allegiance," writes Thomas Kelly, "if I could find a Mark worthy to be the aim of the bow of my life, I should gladly pull the arrow back to its head and let all fly upon a single shot."

Did you ever thrill with the desire to venture forth with sublime audacity? Did you ever wish to "bet your life" on God, and yet it seemed you had no place to go and no armour for the battle?

In ancient times there was usually one trumpeter and one light-bearer for each army of several hundred men. The trumpeters and light-bearers stood back while the army moved forward to do battle.

Now prayer is like that. The man who prays cannot always lead in the fight. And yet prayer scatters the forces of evil faster and more completely than *any* mere action can do! That is the lesson of Gideon.

Oh, do not be ashamed if you seem chained and impotent when the enemy approaches and the darkness deepens! Just light your torches and blow your trumpets and stand every man in his place of prayer.

Our dear heavenly Father, though forces of evil about us be legion, let Thy power of Love scatter them as dust before the wind. Amen.

And when the servant of the man of God was risen early, and gone forth, behold, an host compassed the city both with horses and chariots. And his servant said unto him, Alas, my master! how shall we do? And he answered, Fear not: For they that be with us are more than they that be with them. And Elisha prayed, and said, Lord, I pray thee, open his eyes, that he may see. And the Lord opened the eyes of the young man; and he saw: and, behold, the mountain was full of horses and chariots of fire round about Elisha. (2 Kings 6 : 15–17)

You and Those You Love Are One

Y ou love that which belongs to you, is a part of you, is identical with you. To love something or someone means to take it unto yourself, assimilate it into yourself in spirit, and make it a part of yourself. What you love you actually become. Love Light and you become Light. Love Love and you become like Love; you spread Love. Continue to love Love and you finally become Love itself. As God is Love, to love Love in yourself or in others is the highest thing you can do.

To love a person or a thing means to realize your UNITY with the person or the thing you love. Now the sense of Love and the sense of unity can never come on a low or materialistic plane. Love and unity are in essence spiritual terms. Realize your unity with anything and it simply means you are lifted to the realm of spirit, and the spirit of the thing meets your spirit.

Now the SPIRIT of anything is its essential goodness. For instance, even the spirit of loaning and indebtedness is good. The spirit which makes possible the loan and debt is Trust. So when you go out to pay a debt which has heretofore seemed a nightmare to you, you will meet the Trust which was behind it.

And when your love for a person is so perfect and complete that you and he are one, then you are in heaven on earth.

> And the glory which thou gavest me I have given them; that they may be one, even as we are one: I in them, and thou in me, that they may be made perfect in one; and that the world may know that thou hast sent me, and hast loved them, as thou hast loved me. (John 17 : 22–23)

We Find Each Other

I BELIEVE that God has selected those persons who are to belong to my life's Plan, and through proximity, mutual attraction or need we are continually finding each other out. I believe in praying for ever-increasing capacity to love and serve, and for greater worthiness to be loved and served by others.

I believe in asking my Heavenly Father for those things which are mine according to the Providential Plan. Thus I am relieved of all anxieties and uncertainties, all jealousy and resentment. I have faith and courage to do my work, whatever it may be, with no thought of the rewards.

I realize that if I try to measure what others are or are not receiving according to their Divine Plan, I minimize my own power to receive blessings.

I believe that when I am hindered from receiving what I desire or doing what I wish to do, God closes the door. And on every closed door there is a sign pointing to another door just ahead, with far greater blessings and opportunities inside.

I believe that only my own blindness, deafness and disobedience cut me off from God, and that God uses the resulting trouble and failure to help me find the inspiration, guidance and power I need to overcome my weakness.

I shall ask my Heavenly Father and Friend, who dwells within me and who has given me this vision of life, to help me to realize it more and more fully every day, and to share with others the peace and joy which are mine.

For as many as are led by the Spirit of God, they are the sons of God. For ye have not received the spirit of bondage again to fear ; but ye have received the Spirit of adoption, whereby we cry, Abba, Father. The Spirit itself beareth witness with our spirit, that we are the children of God : And if children, then heirs ; heirs of God, and joint-heirs with Christ ; if so be that we suffer with him, that we may be also glorified together. (Romans 8 : 14–17)

The Kingdom of Heaven is Within

IN HEAVEN, whenever you wish to be with a person, at that moment he also desires to be with you, and instantly you are together. When you crave another, those about you vanish instantly to fulfil similar desires of their own, and you are left with the one you need at the moment.

In heaven, whenever you wish to express beautiful ideas to make others happier, exactly the right inspiration will come to you, or it will come to others who will immediately pass it to you.

It is this coming and going of blessed persons, this coming and going of blessed ideas, this perfect synchronization of desire and fulfilment, that makes life one perfect symphony. It is more beautiful than sound alone can produce, or light or colour or perfume. For this is a whole symphony of souls, a symphony of love and wisdom and happiness—the perfect synchronization of your inmost being with all other beings. It is that which makes heaven the immeasurably beautiful place that it is—the abode of perfect fulfilment and bliss.

This heaven may be discovered whenever a man turns to God—utterly, completely. Its faint forecast is shown wherever love overcomes hate, and humility overcomes pride, and charity overcomes greed. It begins way down here on earth. So, take it wherever you go—bear the good tidings that the Kingdom of Heaven is at hand, that it begins within you.

> And when he was demanded of the Pharisees, when the kingdom of God should come, he answered them and said, The kingdom of God cometh not with observation: Neither shall they say, Lo here! or, lo there! for, behold, the kingdom of God is within you. (Luke 17: 20–21)

Is it a Safe Hit?

Many ball-players will say that they know when they are making a skilful play BY THE JOY WHICH THRILLS THEM JUST BEFORE THE ACCOMPLISHMENT. A great basketball player once told me that he knew when the ball left his fingertips whether or not he had made a basket. Baseball players often know at the instant their bat meets the ball whether or not they have made a safe hit. Golfers know too, when the club first contacts the ball, whether the stroke is right. In every case an inner joy takes rise before they make the play and extends for some time afterward. So it would seem that joy begins with a subconscious sensation of perfect mind and muscle co-ordination, and actually makes possible the perfect result of the physical effort.

With prayer it is the same. The more joy one can put into prayer—joy based on unselfish, God-conscious thought, and not an ephemeral thing of "self"—the more quickly will come the reward or manifestation of God's answer to prayer. For joy binds man to God and it is by joy, born of a certainty about the greatest Realities, that man is forever united to that which is good. So often is this immediate sense of joy the accompaniment of the answer to prayer that it is difficult to know whether that sense is the cause or the sign of fulfilment. Probably it is both ; joy synchronizes with the answer and is, so to speak, the partner of fulfilment, while the primary inner realization that we are one with God inspires the joy that passes our understanding.

These things have I spoken unto you, that my joy might remain in you, and that your joy might be full. (John 15 : 11)

You Can Overcome Fear

ARE you afraid of water, fire, thunderstorms or some animal? Then discover your unity with it and it cannot harm you. To discover the underlying unity of all creatures and natural forces, and to realize their significance in the divine scheme for the universe, is to raise your thoughts from *things* to the *spirit* of Oneness behind all creation. Thus you overcome the general effect of seemingly dangerous elements, by rising above the ideas of the average race-mind.

Love and Unity are the only paths leading upward from things and personalities to ideas and spirit. In short, Love and Unity take us from the carnal to the spiritual realm of living.

The early Greeks gave a " god " to every element apparently beyond their control. For instance, when a Greek set out on a journey by boat he first saluted the god of Water and the god of Travel. Thus, in his child-like, crude way he discovered a unity with natural forces and overcame his fears before he began the journey. Such faith has sustained men of simple belief through all kinds of dangers.

Now we know there is no other God, but the Father. And when we realize our unity with *all* that He has ever created, we discover our unity with Him is perfect and complete and nothing can separate us from goodness. Fear is overcome the moment we begin to *rise above* our instinctive concept of things, and attain a consciousness of God's ever-present Love and Power and His Will to keep us in perfect peace, as we live and move among creatures and influences that belong on the earth.

For the Lord is a great God, and a great King above all gods. In his hand are the deep places of the earth; the strength of the hills is his also. The sea is his, and he made it; and his hands formed the dry land. O come, let us worship and bow down: let us kneel before the Lord our Maker. For he is our God; and we are the people of his pasture, and the sheep of his hand. (Psalm 95 : 3–7)

He Walks With Me and He Talks With Me

Try taking a Three-mile Jaunt with God!

The first mile should be dedicated to achieving a perfectly blank and relaxed mind. Just swing along at an easy pace, in rhythm with the whole universe about you, and looking only where it is natural to gaze, with no purpose whatever except to become as UNSELF-conscious as possible. Look up at the sky or out at the world, and feel that solid undergirding of earth beneath your feet.

Now the second mile should be dedicated to renewal and recuperation. Feel the thrill of new life flowing through your veins. Enjoy the health you feel in every responsive muscle. Breathe deeply—not only of the air, but space as well. And dwell on any ideas which come to you naturally and gladly, but only on these. For you are to enjoy to the fullest the experience of walking with God, your head held high and balanced happily on top of a straight spine!

The third mile will be dedicated to inspiration. Open all the windows of your soul. Look upward with joy to God and outward with love to all your fellow men. And your mind, made blank the first mile and clean and happy the second, will be a receiving set for God's truest and divinest inspirations. You need not judge or check any of your concepts now. They will come in perfect sequence and perfect order, for God will reveal to you a pattern for your life in terms of His Divine Plan. When you reach home you will know He is truly " closer than breathing and nearer than hands and feet."

Make a joyful noise unto the Lord, all ye lands. Serve the Lord with gladness ; come before his presence with singing. Know ye that the Lord he is God : it is he that hath made us, and not we ourselves : we are his people, and the sheep of his pasture. Enter into his gates with thanksgiving, and into his courts with praise : be thankful unto him, and bless his name. For the Lord is good ; his mercy is everlasting ; and his truth endureth to all generations. (Psalm 100)

Time and Space

WHEN we abide in such stillness that everything we do is free of selfconscious effort we make a great discovery: Time and Space are two toys which God has given to man, and man uses them to amuse himself while he waits outside the Garden of Heaven. Whenever we put on the coloured glasses of Space our entire life on earth appears to be a constantly moving process; whenever we put on the coloured glasses of Time our life on earth appears to be a constantly growing process. Through the lens of Time everything seems to be growing and decaying; through the lens of Space everything appears to be coming and going.

But are the angels in heaven pestered by all this coming and going? Are they bothered by all this growing and decaying?

Suppose for a moment we took off the spectacles of Time and Space and saw the world as the angels see it: a simple Temple in the midst of Infinity and Eternity. It would then be revealed that all the Love which ever was, is, or will be exists at this very moment, is everywhere present and is instantly available whenever we need it and seek it. It would be revealed that all the friends we need or crave are seeking us. And we should discover that all the sunshine we need is already pouring out continually through the solar rays, all the gas and oil and coal is already under our feet waiting to be mined, and every poem, symphony and sonata is deep in the mind of mankind, instantly available when the poet or composer calls for them.

True, these riches within ourselves or within the earth or within others do not come at every haphazard call. They await some inner, inscrutable Plan worked out in the blueprints of the Master Planner. When we yield ourselves to the Divine Plan of this Master Planner all things seem able to come to us in perfect sequence and perfect order, in exactly the right way, at exactly the right time. As Catherine Mendenhall writes: " Time is a Teacher; and Space is a Friend to keep us from travelling too fast and too far. We have to learn Patience and then we can blend with the Time and the Place wherever we are."

> But they that wait upon the Lord shall renew their strength; they shall mount up with wings as eagles; they shall run, and not be weary; and they shall walk, and not faint. (Isaiah 40: 31)

The Way of Love

Do not keep for yourself the persons who come to you with their love. Unbind them, let them go, teach them to recognize only the mastery of God and to yield only to His desires and leadings. You have the power to give away those persons who give themselves to you—who have given you their love. So dare to love and to be loved, but dare to relinquish, too!

For if we try to keep for our own private, personal aggrandizement—no matter how subtly—the love of others, then jealousy, tyranny and all manner of suffering will result. But if we allow others to love us, as channels through which their love may flow straight back to the Heart of the Father, we cannot ever lose or hurt them.

One who loves in the way I am describing, who does not want to possess his friends or loved ones for any selfish purposes, finds that he possesses them after all—for larger purposes. And they who are possessed by a love as limitless and powerful as that which I am describing are set free, for such love removes all limitations to their growth and enables them to meet any need. It is the Holy Spirit manifesting through clear souls.

And here is a great eternal Truth: EVERYONE DEEP DOWN IN HIS SOUL LONGS TO BE POSSESSED BY A TOWERING, COLOSSAL, UNSELFISH, UNSELF-SEEKING LOVE. That is the aim and purpose of his entire life's journey. To find such love is to find the very Kingdom itself here and now. For then we abide in the Father in whom only is Love Complete.

> Jesus saith unto her, Mary! She turned herself, and saith unto him, Rabboni! which is to say, Master. Jesus saith unto her, Touch me not; for I am not yet ascended to my Father: but go to my brethren, and say unto them, I ascend unto my Father, and your Father; and to my God, and your God. (John 20: 16–17)

You Are a Branch on the Vine

As we are branches and Christ is the Vine, the most important decision that we must make in life is the choice of position we shall take in relation to the Vine. Shall we keep our consciousness, our awareness, where the branch connects with the Vine, or out at the tip far from the source of our supply, and live there exposed to every wind of emotion and desire?

When a man chooses to take his stand with the true " I " that is united with his God, miracles begin to occur round him. This is because he lives, moves and has his being in the creative, Godlike part of his nature, instead of the created, manifest, human side. People may acknowledge the miracles gratefully and celebrate, advertise or even exploit them. But often they will turn upon the man himself and condemn him as a fanatic leading orthodox flocks astray.

Father, may our lives be hid with Christ in Thee. May our thoughts, our will, our hopes, be Thine. In humility and sincerity we regret our efforts to defend Thee with condemnation toward any who are not yet comforted by Thy blessing. May Christ's redemptive Love and his matchless Grace blot these transgressions on our part from the book of Thy remembrance, so we may start afresh each day as newborn children of our Father, heirs and co-heirs of Thy beloved Son, brothers and partners with mankind.

May the aching open wounds of our spirits be healed by the heavenly transfusions of Christ's blood, mercifully restoring the years that the locusts have eaten. May His love and His joy flow through us until we are healed by a perfect welding, as branches to the Vine. Then, Beloved Father, we thank Thee for the peace that passeth understanding of men, the peace when we are one with Thee. Make us Thy chosen and ordained apostles to draw others, through the sincerity of our words, the genuineness of our Love and the contagion of our Joy, into blessed oneness with Thee.

Verily, verily, I say unto you, He that believeth on me, the works that I do shall he do also ; and greater works than these shall he do ; because I go unto my Father. (John 14 : 12)

130

Blessed Are the Merciful

ENTER any church and you will find some spotless souls who are so rigidly righteous, so immune to temptation, that they find it very difficult to be merciful to those who are weak, neurotic, or easily led into temptation. You will also find some rather loose characters—men who have sinned frequently and yet are more popular than their stiff-necked and righteous brethren simply because, being sinners themselves, they can understand weakness in others. They do not judge or condemn ; but their uncritical attitude is not particularly redemptive because they have not yet overcome their own temptations.

However, when a really righteous man can include within his own rigid code of morals a spirit of mercy and forgiveness toward weaker brethren, he becomes the finest and most redemptive personality in the church, for then he is truly pure in heart. The combination of righteousness and mercy provides the spiritual perception by which we SEE GOD, at least in the face of our fellow men.

If we ask God to make us righteous without asking Him to give us mercy, our righteousness will be a sterile virtue. If we are merciful to others who are downfallen but continue to indulge in sins ourselves, our mercy will be sterile. But if we hunger and thirst after righteousness for ourselves while we extend the hand of fellowship and compassion to the sinner, we can bring permanent redemption to others. To see what is God-like in a sinner is to be truly PURE IN HEART.

> The Lord is merciful and gracious, slow to anger, and plenteous in mercy. . . . He hath not dealt with us after our sins ; nor rewarded us according to our iniquities. For as the heaven is high above the earth, so great is his mercy toward them that fear him. As far as the east is from the west, so far hath he removed our transgressions from us. (Psalm 103 : 8–12)

I Will Repay, Saith the Lord

IN Hawaii, if a Kahoona puts a curse on one, the evil he forecasts will come to pass if the victim sends out thoughts of fear or hate toward the Kahoona. These create a bridge over which the curse of the other achieves its evil purpose all the more easily. If, on the other hand, the victim sends forth love toward his enemy, the love creates a protective wall against which the evil curse breaks without avail, and if it is not withdrawn, it boomerangs back upon the sender.

Jesus was not a " sissy " or a " pussyfooter " when He said " forgive your enemies, do good to those who persecute you." He was releasing the most powerful weapon, both for defence of the attacked and for discipline of the attacker. If the latter continues the attack, it boomerangs in the form of punishment ; if he repents, it brings him conversion and salvation. When Stephen was martyred by Saul's men, he said, " Lord, hold not this against them," thus releasing powers that brought Saul to his knees as a slave of Christ.

Following the partition in Palestine the Arabs were driven out of their homes, leaving all their property and belongings behind them. With no lodgings but caves and tents on the Jordan side, their hearts were filled with bitterness and hate. Similar hate fills the hearts of the Jews. Neither of these groups believes in Jesus so the situation is very serious. It creates what is known as " the Palestine problem." If either side could take the daring step of forgiving their enemies and asking the Lord to take charge of the situation, a solution could be worked out. This tragic situation merely dramatizes on a large scale many smaller situations that exist in your life and mine.

Bless those who persecute you ; bless and do not curse them. . . . Beloved, never avenge yourselves, but leave it to the wrath of God ; for it is written, " Vengeance is mine, I will repay, says the Lord." No, " if your enemy is hungry, feed him ; if he is thirsty, give him drink ; for by so doing you will heap burning coals upon his head." Do not be overcome by evil, but overcome evil with good. (Romans 12 : 14, 19–21, R.S.V.)

134

Faith and the Mountain

WHERE two or three come together and symphonize ("agree" comes from the word "symphonize"), asking anything in His Name, their prayers will be answered, even to the extent of lifting a mountain and casting it into the sea. And remember that mountains of hate and fear are as gigantic and apparently immovable as rock and soil.

The physical and spiritual realms, in the past considered so far apart, are alike in all important respects. For instance, the smaller and more invisible a thing is, the more powerful it can be. And the more completely and harmoniously the invisible elements unite with each other, the greater the power released from their union. Compare the infinitesimal uranium atom with a gigantic rocky mountain; one does not ever appear to the naked eye while the other appears massively before us. Yet the energies within that atom could blast a mountain away!

The world of science *knows* about the power of invisible elements. Does the world of religion know it as well? Scientists have unwavering faith in the laws of physical forces, such as the law of gravity, the law of the tides, the law of electricity. Do religious folk have the same unwavering faith in the great laws of soul force, such as the law of sacrifice, the law of humility, the law of love? In giving the beatitudes of the Sermon on the Mount, Jesus spoke with that confident assurance which a scientist has to-day when he talks of the laws of science. Do we share Jesus' confidence in the laws of the spirit? Do we act upon those laws which He gave us? Do we know the power of Love and Joy—the divine blessings produced by Faith?

> Whosoever therefore shall break one of these least commandments, and shall teach men so, he shall be called the least in the kingdom of heaven: but whosoever shall do and teach them, the same shall be called great in the kingdom of heaven. (Matthew 5 : 19)

There is Healing in Laughter

WHEN God blessed us with the imagination to see harmonies and congruities and logical relationships in this life, He blessed us also with a sense of humour to see the inharmonies, incongruities and illogical relationships—and smile. Humour enables us to think without malice or fear; rather, it transforms malice or fear by giving us diversion, change, enjoyment, to enrich our store of human experience. Thus inharmony, incongruity and illogical relationships become assets for us instead of liabilities.

A teacher can eradicate a pupil's mistake more quickly and effectively with laughter of a gentle kind than by punishment. Doctors can cure trivial complaints with humour better than with drugs.

But by humour and laughter we do not of course mean the low, coarse type of buffoonery. We mean exalted, heartfelt joy, laughter compounded of love and gratitude to God. This is divine laughter, which echoes throughout heaven and takes us tripping higher and higher up the mountain-sides. The more evil we see and the more trouble which comes upon us, the more we can laugh with love and joy, until at last we come to that stage where evil and trouble cannot possibly overtake us. For, as the touch of Midas converted everything into gold, so can the touch of heavenly laughter convert shadows into golden bits of sunshine to brighten every path before us.

Then was our mouth filled with laughter, and our tongue with singing : then said they among the heathen, the Lord hath done great things for them. The Lord hath done great things for us ; whereof we are glad. ... They that sow in tears shall reap in joy. He that goeth forth and weepeth, bearing precious seed, shall doubtless come again with rejoicing, bringing his sheaves with him. (Psalm 126 : 2–3, 5–6)

First Things First

IN ANY church which is properly wired for electricity, no effort is required to bring light into the rooms. There are no smoky lampshades to clean, no paraffin to pour and no wicks to keep carefully trimmed. Just by the flick of a switch the whole building can be flooded with light.

And so it is in any church which is properly " wired " spiritually ; no effort is required to bring the Light of Christ to the congregation. When the minister is selflessly and utterly surrendered to God, the elders, deacons, trustees, superintendents, directors of activities, etc., are perhaps only slightly less consecrated, and the congregation itself is harmonious with mutual trust and love; the flame of God is already lighted in every heart.

It is not even necessary to put on bazaars and suppers, or advertise in the local papers, to draw a congregation to such a House of God. It is hardly necessary to preach sermons! Merely to step inside the sanctuary, where First Things are really put first, is like stepping into the quietude and harmony of heaven.

One thing have I desired of the Lord, that will I seek after ; that I may dwell in the house of the Lord all the days of my life, to behold the beauty of the Lord, and to inquire in his temple. For in the time of trouble he shall hide me in his pavilion : in the secret of his tabernacle shall he hide me ; he shall set me up upon a rock. And now shall mine head be lifted up above mine enemies round about me : therefore will I offer in his tabernacle sacrifices of joy ; I will sing, yea, I will sing praises unto the Lord. (Psalm 27 : 4–6)

We Are Children of a King

How I have pounded and hammered away at myself trying to melt the hardened metal of my own heart into the softness and pliancy of a little child! How I have argued and expounded and exhorted my friends to turn and become as little children, and how often to no avail! The only way I have consistently succeeded is when I caught myself or others unawares, seated round a camp fire or looking into the calm waters of a lake or ocean, and spontaneously retold familiar fairy stories handed down through the generations by just such retelling. A fairy story performs a sort of painless operation on our subconscious minds. It administers a sort of anæsthesia to our cynical, guarded and menacingly logical reasoning processes. Then it opens hidden passageways, blocked in the days of our youth, which lead back to childhood's joys and enthusiasms and awareness —to the fresh and simple attitudes to life's newness.

One of my favourite fairy tales is "Jack and the Beanstalk," and to me it is one of the most real documents of human life. For we are all sons of a King, and we spend our lives trading beans for cattle or cattle for beans. We all have an opportunity at some time to climb beanstalks and cope with giants. Some of us have known the thrill of catching the goose that lays a golden egg whenever we need one, and the harp which sings through our minds the right ideas at the right times, and seem always to be where we wish to be with the people we wish to have with us. And to think that all of these blessings can be ours when we turn and become as a little child!

Oh, there are volumes to write about fairy tales and their parable interpretations which teach the greatest truths to the subconscious mind. And yet we must leave even fairy stories behind us if we are to make the final ascent to the Kingdom. For only the Holy Scriptures lead to the superconscious realms of Christian revelation where our vision is Christ's, and the Kingdom of Heaven the only Reality.

And a little child shall lead them. (Isaiah 11 : 6)

Pray for the New Age

OUR children ask, " Will bombs fall on our city ? " According to history the answer would be : " The Thirty Years War of the Middle Ages almost destroyed Europe, thirty years of war in this century have already threatened civilization, and another thirty years of war would destroy the world."

Society knows it must become an integrated whole in order to survive, and has been making all sorts of attempts to achieve a degree of wholeness according to various philosophies and purposes. The Mediterranean Age glimpsed wholeness in the world of Truth for one brief moment in Aristotelian philosophy, medieval art caught the spirit in its world of Beauty, and the Roman Church presented the concept in terms of Goodness. But the Good, True and Beautiful have never been integrated long enough to withstand eruptions from outside and corruptions from within and many foundations have crumbled.

The Atlantic Age, attempting to capture wholeness with imperialism, made inroads into the jungle to harness human labour, and then conceived out of savage materialism marvellous mechanical extensions to the human hand and brain.

The victory march after the Second World War was a swan song for Europe, as world leadership shifted to Russia and the United States.

The Mediterranean Age is dead, the Atlantic Age is dying, and the Pacific Age has begun. Are we going to establish a whole world now, based upon a sound philosophy acceptable to both east and west even though that could not be achieved by building upon the dreams of a Karl Marx nor yet of a J. P. Morgan ? Or shall we continue the argument until bombs and other fantastic weapons furnished by the Atlantic Age shatter all dreams into eternal silence ?

I would let Jesus answer the children :

> For God sent not his Son into the world to condemn the world ; but that the world through him might be saved. (John 3 : 17)

144

Only God Can Make a Tree

LOOK at the tree there in the clearing. To most it is only a tree. It is speaking no speech with its uplifted branches and its many-tongued leaves. To most the tree begins and ends at a certain place and that is all. The true seer knows that where the visible leaves and branches cease, there the true tree begins. The real tree draws up from the earth strange nutrition beyond our understanding ; it draws down from the sun the substance of light and moisture from the passing air. Despite our much speaking we understand all this as little as did the remotest savage.

The real life of the tree is in the sun and hardly at all in the visible branches. Cut off the sun rays and the tree is dead, much more completely dead than if you merely cut off the branches. Yes, the life of the tree is in the sun. The tree, as it stretches its limbs toward the sky and sinks its roots into the earth, says, " I am a part of all that I have met. I am a part of earth and sky. I, by reaching upward, unite earth and sky. I hold the earth in the grasp of my roots and I uphold the sky in my antlered branches. I stand between two eternities, linking the infinite and the finite."

For as the rain cometh down, and the snow from heaven, and returneth not thither, but watereth the earth, and maketh it bring forth and bud, that it may give seed to the sower, and bread to the eater : So shall my word be that goeth forth out of my mouth : it shall not return unto me void, but it shall accomplish that which I please, and it shall prosper in the thing whereto I sent it. For ye shall go out with joy, and be led forth with peace : the mountains and the hills shall break forth before you into singing, and all the trees of the field shall clap their hands. Instead of the thorn shall come up the fir tree, and instead of the brier shall come up the myrtle tree : and it shall be to the Lord for a name, for an everlasting sign that shall not be cut off. (Isaiah 55 : 10–13)

There Is No Death

WILL you forgive me for making this meditation somewhat personal ? Read again my introduction to this book, in which I affirm my conviction that death is but a doorway to fuller living and greater service and that in heaven our soul's sincere desires are multiplied in power by infinity.

For six months the parents and grandfather of Mary Lou Elliott watched their little girl fade out of this world, stricken with leukaemia. Although Mary Lou did not know that she was on the last journey, her chief delight during those months was to contemplate the kind of joys only heaven can give. She was such a perfectionist that earthly life with its limitations could not be compared with the wonders of heaven.

When she passed away at three o'clock one morning I was two thousand miles from her, but at that moment I suddenly wakened with the realization that Mary Lou had stepped into the arms of God. Only those who have given away an only son, or as I did, an only granddaughter, can fully comprehend the sacrificial love of God who gave His only begotten Son that the world through Him might be saved. That early morning I experienced an absolutely overwhelming sense of oneness with my Father who had taken Mary Lou to Himself.

Three months later when I went home I found my daughter Marion and my son-in-law Norman so marvellously sustained that their courage and peace were a living inspiration to all their friends. And I told them, " I can just see Mary Lou now, looking carefully all over heaven for just the right little girl to help fill the void she has left." Eleven months later little Kathleen Elliott was born, and a prettier, brighter-eyed laughing girl I have never seen ! How I love to tell her about the sister she will not see on earth who will always be blessing her from heaven.

And now when I need strength or inspiration I can go back down the corridors of time to that Upper Room and hear Jesus promise :

> He that believeth on me, the works that I do shall he do also ; and greater works than these shall he do ; because I go unto my Father. (John 14 : 12)

Jesus Is Real

Jesus is real! And nothing henceforth can take Him from me. Since Jesus has stepped out of the world in the body, His presence is here more apparently than ever before. Though He has vanished from our earthly sight, He will never vanish from our heavenly gaze. Only to lift our eyes high enough, only to yearn in our hearts toward Him greatly enough, and He will be in our midst. And as we become aware of it and get quiet in the contemplation of it, that Presence becomes more penetrating until it is overwhelming in its power. Everyone we meet becomes so lovely and dear that we wonder how such a heaven can exist on earth.

Even mistakes become precious and valuable. The denial by Peter in the courtyard and the wistful yearning that followed become as beautiful as a pearl set in a ring of gold. Even Judas' betrayal and the agonizing remorse that drove him to a rope on a lonely tree take on the aspects of a mother giving birth to her child. The agony of Mother Mary at the foot of the cross as her Son was projected into heaven was more magnificent than her agony in the manger as her Babe was projected into this world. It was precious for a child to be born in a manger; it was more precious for a God to be born on a cross.

> Do ye inquire among yourselves of that I said, A little while, and ye shall not see me : and again, a little while, and ye shall see me ? Verily, verily, I say unto you, that ye shall weep and lament, but the world shall rejoice : and ye shall be sorrowful, but your sorrow shall be turned into joy. A woman when she is in travail hath sorrow, because her hour is come : but as soon as she is delivered of the child, she remembereth no more the anguish, for joy that a man is born into the world. And ye now therefore have sorrow : but I will see you again, and your heart shall rejoice, and your joy no man taketh from you. (John 16: 19–22)

Ask, Seek and Knock

THINK of Christ as though He could walk with you, talk with you, put His arm about your shoulder. Think of Him standing behind you while you work, or accompanying you while you play. Ask Him to be your pilot when you fly in a plane, your engineer when you ride a train, your driver in a car. Perhaps it will be hours after you have made such a conscious effort that you will be aware that CHRIST ACTUALLY WAS THERE. For He is Spirit; He is everywhere. How can He possibly avoid you?

At night just before you retire know that Christ is standing by your bed, ready to guard you—yes, to guard even your subconscious dreams and thoughts. And because He is everywhere ask Him to stand at the bedside of the persons you love. Ask Him to put His hand on the fevered brow of the lonely, bewildered one, to take into His arms the pain-racked body, to restore souls and minds and bodies to the wholeness that manifests in health and joy and fruitful living. Then ask Christ to stand at the bedside of persons who hate you, revile you and say all manner of evil against you falsely—to bring them surcease from pain, purification and renewed understanding.

God needs our faith; Christ needs to be called before He can answer. "Ask, seek and knock!" He commands. Yet He is gentle and patient and willing to wait so that His coming may be acknowledged and our faith renewed by His presence.

Teach us, O Father, to love Thee more and more. Make our love for Thee a fountain springing up into eternal life. Make for us a new understanding, Lord, until Thy nearness is an enveloping atmosphere in which we live and move and have our being.

Jesus saith unto him, Thomas, because thou hast seen me, thou hast believed: blessed are they that have not seen, and yet have believed. (John 20 : 29)

God Lights the Way

WE know, O Father, that man is not responsible for making plans,
For Thou art the only Designer
And plans must grow as flowers and trees, from the seed and the acorn.
They must have roots, ramifications, and interweavings
As beautiful as tapestries, as permanent as the eternal stars.
Keep our eye single, our vision clear as light,
That the radiance of Thy infinite Love may shine always on the paths before us,
Revealing all the beauties and wonders ;
And that we may see ourselves as we are—
Thy children, made in Thy image and likeness,
The perfect expression of Thy perfect direction,
Each moment conscious of Thy perfect ideas in perfect succession.
As Thou keepest the stars in their courses
So wilt Thou guide our steps in sequence, without interference of any kind
When we keep our trust in Thee ;
When we acknowledge Thee in all our ways
Thou wilt direct our paths.
For Thou art the God of Love,
Giver of every good and perfect gift,
And there is none beside Thee.
Thou art omnipotent, omniscient, omnipresent,
In all, through all, and over all.
Thou art Our God.

Thy word is a lamp unto my feet, and a light unto my path. (Psalm 119 : 105)

The Power of the Sea

I WATCHED the sea surge and pound forward against the rocky ledges with a leisurely, effortless motion—a motion grounded in gravity and governed by the law of the tides. Before me lay four huge rocks and the waves rolled through their crevices like five huge fingers. The fingers seemed to have power enough to clasp and hold the rocks had they cared to do so; or to bend and destroy them. But they did not need to do that. Their gesture of power turned into a caress, as they withdrew. They seemed to feel, " Why should I destroy, or yet cling to, that which is already mine ? "

Here and there cliffs towered up high—too lofty to be reached by the sea, even for a caress. " I don't belong to you, I am above you," they seemed to say. " You shall never possess me! "

To them the sea merely unsheathed its white teeth in a smile that rippled along the whole shore line of the island, and that afternoon the sun sent a rainbow ribbon of light and carried a river of water to the clouds. The next day it fell in torrents down upon those cliffs, sweeping their faces, caressing their stiff necks, and patting them tenderly upon their heads, as though to say, " You cannot escape me after all, O Land! "

Yes, the whole round earth is held in the hollow of the sea's mighty hand. The land, rigid and firm, is possessed and ruled, controlled, and given life by the sea itself because the sea knows how to relax utterly and be utterly obedient to the laws of the tide, of the sun, of the universe.

And little Man, if he gives himself completely to the great laws of the spirit and of life, to the tides and the sun, perhaps he too may hold the world in the hollow of his hand.

> Where wast thou when I laid the foundations of the earth ? declare, if thou hast understanding. . . . or who shut up the sea with doors, when it brake forth, as if it had issued out of the womb ? . . . Hast thou entered into the springs of the sea ? Or hast thou walked in the search of the depth ? (Job 38 : 4, 8, 16)

Hind's Feet

YEARS ago a great revelation came to me as I pondered a strange statement in the Bible : " He maketh my feet like hind's feet and setteth me upon my high places." No animal has such perfect correlation of its front and rear feet as the female deer or the hind. And this was the blinding revelation : As the feet of the hind are to the mountain-sides, so is the mind of man to the heights of living ; and as the rear feet of the hind are to its front feet, so is the subconscious mind of man to his conscious mind. And as the creature with the most perfect correlation of front and rear feet is the surest to reach the mountain-top in safety, so a person with the most perfect correlation between his conscious and his subconscious mind is sure to reach the heights of living.

Our lips speak the thoughts of our conscious minds, but only the heart speaks the thoughts of our subconscious mind. " As a man thinketh *in his heart*, so is he." " Out of the heart come the issues of life." And when the lips and the heart are aligned, when they " track " together with the absolute sureness of the hind's feet tracking together, then nothing is impossible—whether it be the climbing of mountains or the casting of mountains into the sea.

Ask yourself how many things you have done in your life, with all your strength, all your mind, all your heart, and all your soul. In other words, how often have you tracked " with all four feet " ?

The world, the church, the community, the family, and every individual needs the leadership of persons who have learned to track sure-footedly in high places. To climb with hind's feet one's eye must be single, one's heart must be single, one's faith must be sure.

The light of the body is the eye : if therefore thine eye be single, thy whole body shall be full of light. . . . No man can serve two masters : for either he will hate the one, and love the other ; or else he will hold to the one, and despise the other. Ye cannot serve God and mammon. (Matthew 6 : 22, 24)

Prayer for the Church

JESUS said of Peter, " Upon this rock I will build my church." And yet after such a tremendous statement of faith in one man the Master himself predicted Peter would deny him three times in one night.

Though the Church was founded upon the Rock, it has denied Christ in three ways, the same ways that Peter denied Him even before the night of betrayal.

By largely avoiding a healing ministry the Church reflects Peter's inadequacy to cope with the problem of the epileptic boy, whose father told Jesus : " I spake to thy disciples that they should cast him [the dumb spirit] out ; and they could not." Jesus turned to those around Him and cried, " O faithless generation, how long shall I be with you ? how long shall I suffer you ? " And he cured the boy immediately.

By virtually putting its blessing upon warfare as a means of settling international disputes, the Church follows Peter's example of angrily slicing off the ear of the servant who accosted his Master. Yet Jesus commanded Peter to put back his sword, and healed the ear of his " enemy." That night He gave himself up to the forces of evil yet He later prayed from the Cross : " Father, forgive them, for they know not what they do."

By avoiding reference to many of the most vital problems in our society —such as alcoholism, racial prejudice, economic injustice, and political corruption—the Church has tried to protect its leaders from public criticism and argument. When Peter begged Jesus to save Himself and turn away from Jerusalem, the young Master replied, " Get thee behind me, Satan : thou art an offence unto me : for thou savourest not the things that be of God, but those that be of men."

After His resurrection Jesus appeared to Peter and gave him the opportunity to cancel out his denials with three amending affirmations. We in our churches may receive the same forgiveness for past weakness and begin to prove our faith.

> Therefore whosoever heareth these sayings of mine, and doeth them, I will liken him unto a wise man, which built his house upon a rock : And the rain descended, and the floods came, and the winds blew, and beat upon that house ; and it fell not : for it was founded upon a rock. And every one that heareth these sayings of mine, and doeth them not, shall be likened unto a foolish man, which built his house upon the sand : And the rain descended, and the floods came, and the winds blew, and beat upon that house ; and it fell : and great was the fall of it. (Matthew 7 : 24–27)

What Are You?

You attract unto yourself not the condition you ask, not the condition you expect, not the condition you want; but you attract unto yourself the condition that accords with what you are.

Are you a *giving* person? Then the world will give much to you. Are you a *getting* person? Then the world will get much away from you.

> Do you give powerfully? Then power will come to you.
> Do you give lovingly? Then love will come to you.
> Do you give beautifully? Then beauty will come to you.
> Do you give abundantly? Then abundance will come to you.

What shall you give? Most beautiful, most powerful, most wonderful of all gifts is yourself—your faith, your trust, your love. Trust men, trust God, trust events.

Do not *have* love. *Be* love. And then you will attract all the goodness, all the perfection that the world has in store for you; you will draw the very Kingdom of heaven itself down to the earth. When your power to love becomes like God's power to love, then your power to create will become like God's power to create.

And the moment that you become Love, thenceforth

> Whatever you ask shall be yours.
> Whatever you expect shall be yours.
> Whatever you want shall be yours.

For thenceforth you shall ask for, and expect and want only that which is in accord with the spirit of infinite Love.

For as he thinketh in his heart, so is he. (Proverbs 23 : 7)

Fanner-Bee Christians

I T WAS a glorious night of midsummer. A moon at full and a host of stars lit the old bee garden with a soft crystalline light, while ever so slight a breeze tipped the treetops. At the door of one of the hives the old bee-keeper came to a stop, and we listened to a sound like distant sea waves, advancing and retreating. It was a sibilant note, and persistent.

" Those are the fanner-bees at work," whispered the bee-keeper. " It is their job to keep the hive sweet and fresh. They are standing inside with their heads lowered, facing the centre of the hive. Their wings are moving so rapidly that if you could see in, you would think they were just a grey mist. These bees draw out the bad air through one side of the hive while pure air is sucked in from the other."

As I stood listening to the fanner-bees I felt strangely close to one of nature's great wonders—the mystery of bee life. The old bee-keeper lit a candle and held it near the hive. Instantly the light went out, extinguished by the strong air current. Those infinitesimal bee wings moving in unison, could make a draught to quench a candle. Think of it!

" If there were enough fanner-bee Christians as keen on their jobs as these bees are on theirs," whispered my friend, " wouldn't the world be sweet and fresh ? "

And I thought of the shut-ins, the aged and invalid, who think their active days of service are past. And I knew that if they could think of themselves as fanner-bees, and could be united in spirit with all others like them in this nation, the power of their prayers would be fabulous!

> And when Jesus was come into Peter's house, he saw his wife's mother laid, and sick of a fever. And he touched her hand, and the fever left her : and she arose, and ministered unto them. (Matthew 8 : 14–15)

My Yoke Is Easy

BECAUSE Jesus hung upon the Cross we do not need to hang upon it. But in this weak and erring world, no one who would help a brother can avoid at times bearing his cross with him. Those of us who do not have the alcoholic's appetite must help the alcoholic. We who were born into homes of love must bear some of the burdens of the criminal born into a house of hate. When we do that, the cross ceases to be a cross and becomes a yoke instead—uniting us in loving service and fellowship with those whom we may help.

Even greater than the promise of immortality, symbolized by the open tomb, is the promise of blessing for the sinner and outcast derived from the Cross of the atoning Christ. Until one understands the law of the Cross, the law of vertical and horizontal pulls, he is illiterate on the subject of humanity. Jesus explained the vertical pull in the words " Love God," and the horizontal pull in the words " Love man." Upon this Cross, or Law, hang all the laws and the prophets. Thus the Cross is the visible symbol of our collective sin and the divine Forgiveness.

All religions incorporate, in some way, the ministry of Love. But only Christianity visions the heights expressed in the Sermon on the Mount. Grace is an attribute of God ; Mercy is an attribute of man. When in our zeal for the Grace of God we blot out our exercise of Mercy toward man, we are " letting the zeal of our house eat us up."

> Come unto me, all ye that labour and are heavy laden, and I will give you rest. Take my yoke upon you, and learn of me ; for I am meek and lowly in heart : and ye shall find rest unto your souls. For my yoke is easy, and my burden is light. (Matthew 11 : 28–30)

In Remembrance of Him

THE first Lord's Supper opened a channel of communion directly with God. We, as disciples of Jesus, have a choice between two ways of using this great event that first occurred two thousand years ago in the Upper Room in Galilee. We may participate in the service as a mere ecclesiastical form, a religious rite, separate from life, which we can enjoy at certain times only. Instead of charging admission, as does a theatre or cinema, we can take up a collection to pay the curator's salary. Or, we may participate in Holy Communion as a vital part of our religious life, experience the cleansing from sin, and become filled with the living Christ.

Too often we good churchgoers bow before the great, incandescent, transfigured Author of the little drama of the Upper Room one day a week, or once a month, and all the other days we forget Him. The far-reaching implications of that event which took place in our church are lost to us as soon as the church doors open and we emerge into the everyday routine of our mundane lives.

Think what would happen in this old world if everyone who partook of the Lord's Supper in the sanctuary would go forth carrying the Light of Christ-consciousness in his soul! That light, shining wherever he went, would inspire others to glorify the Father also. For we have the sacred privilege of renewing contact with the Source of Light and Love at any given moment; Holy Communion is a reminder of that promise.

Take heed that ye do not your alms before men, to be seen of them; otherwise ye have no reward of your Father which is in heaven. (Matthew 6: 1)

Thy Kingdom Come

THROUGH the marvellous working of his subconscious inventive capacity, man has externalized into objectivity all the qualities within his being. Writes Vera Stanley Adler: " He has expressed his emotional and imaginative make-up in picture, in tapestry and in poem. He has externalized every muscle and sinew in his body in the form of tools, machines and engines. He has externalized his eyesight in the form of camera and cinema, his hearing in the form of music, telephone and wireless. At present he is endeavouring to capture in externalized instruments the very cosmic ray forces which play through him. His achievements are incessant, untiring and astonishing."

Jesus said that man may externalize also the soul forces which God channels through him. This He proclaimed in the Gospel. This was the Good News! So, we can externalize upon the outer world an inner peace of mind. But first we must have that peace within ourselves. When enough persons with love and meekness unite in a common desire to be instruments for the creation of a Kingdom of Heaven on earth, it too can come into manifestation.

All legislative bodies which earnestly strive to establish more reasonable justice in the affairs of men deserve our tangible and spiritual support. The United Nations can be an instrument for the creation of a peaceful world, on the government level. But it requires constant undergirding, with our faith and prayers and study and action!

Lord, make me an instrument of Thy will; show me how to bring harmony in high places by establishing harmony in my own home. Give me a vision of Thy Kingdom and a steady gaze so that I may see through the outer manifestations into the hearts of men. O Lord, dissipate the darkness and gloom from all chambers of human debate! Let the Light of Thy Presence clarify our common needs and give us courage to do Thy Will. I am Thy servant, prepared to serve Thee, Master and Ruler of mankind. In Jesus' Name. Amen.

I will put my law in their inward parts, and write it in their hearts; and will be their God, and they shall be my people. (Jeremiah 31 : 33)

The Everlasting Hills

THOUGH the reflection in the water may quiver and ruffle
And conceal Thy great beauty at the beck of the winds and tides,
We know that Thy Truth shall never be moved.
Though discord and misunderstanding may appear in the world below,
We know that if we lift our eyes unto the hills
We shall see Reality is forever clear and beautiful and harmonious.
We know that the more vibration there is from the wind and tide
The more stable and calm stand the everlasting hills.
And the further the mountain tip in the reflection sinks down into the
depths
The higher the dome above it pushes into the heavens.

Give us grace, O God, to see the world of Reality right side up and not
upside down.
May we see the mountain, not the reflection in the pool.
May we see behind every argument the Truth that draws it into Love,
And behind every angry thought the Love that vibrates it into eternal
Harmony.
We pray, O God, that we may look up, and see Thee as Thou art,
And see Man as Thy child, made in Thy perfect and eternal image and
Likeness,
Eternally reflecting Thy Harmony,
Filled with Thy Holy Spirit,
And abiding eternally in Thy Love. Amen.

To whom then will ye liken God? or what likeness will ye compare
unto him? . . . Have ye not known? have ye not heard? hath it not
been told you from the beginning? have ye not understood from the
foundations of the earth? It is he that sitteth upon the circle of the earth,
and the inhabitants thereof are as grasshoppers; that stretcheth out the
heavens as a curtain, and spreadeth them out as a tent to dwell in; That
bringeth the princes to nothing; he maketh the judges of the earth as
vanity. (Isaiah 40 : 18, 21–23)

A Hiding Place

ONCE as I rode by train through a great desert I saw a cow lying out in the blistering sun, and nestled close to her in the shade of her body was a newborn calf. That cow stayed in the intolerable heat to lend comfort to the calf until it would be strong enough to seek shelter in a barn. I recalled Isaiah 32 : 2 : " A man shall be as a hiding place from the wind, and a covert from the tempest ; as rivers of water in a dry place, as the shadow of a great rock in a weary land."

Have you ever been in such desperate trouble that you went seeking help ? And did you find what you needed in some huge, elaborate church made with costly skill, or even in a sermon ? I think if you were in deep distress that you went directly to a man or woman who you believed would " understand " and love you.

Now you too can be a " hiding place " for others! When others come to you for help first make sure that you are not trying to win praise or admiration, financial remuneration or any other benefit whatever. For to mix love with any alloy renders you useless to others. And do not try to " do things " for them or " save their souls." Just get so close to God that His Presence manifests through you in peace and love. Then, like Sir Galahad, you will have the strength of ten because your heart is pure.

If someone comes to you for friendship even more than help you will be able to bless him more because he will be receptive to your love. You cannot force love upon anyone, but when one needs it you can give it in Jesus' Name, which means with perfect purity. Then expect the greatest blessings to come to him according to God's perfect plan, because he " hungered and thirsted " after righteousness and love.

And we have known and believed the love that God hath to us. God is love ; and he that dwelleth in love dwelleth in God, and God in him. Herein is our love made perfect, that we may have boldness in the day of judgment : because as he is, so are we in this world. (1 John 4 : 16–17)

The Soul of the Prophet

THE prophet is one who knows death is a milepost on the Way to life everlasting. He smiles though fortunes vanish, for he sees no limit to the riches of God. He is calm and sweet though friends desert him, for he knows that real Love cannot be taken from him.

A man who has discovered the secret of keeping peace in his soul is worthy to make peace between enemies. Wherever he goes, in whatever circumstances he finds himself, there is within him a healing influence which brings surcease to hate and wars.

Lincoln was a prophet not merely because of his political acumen or brilliant military strategy, but because of the quality of his mercy. These closing words of his inaugural address, the greatest inaugural ever given, express that quality :

" With malice toward none, with charity for all, with firmness in the right as God gives us to see the right, let us strive on to finish the work we are in, to bind up the nation's wounds, to care for him who shall have borne the battle and for his widow and his orphan, to do all which may achieve and cherish a just and lasting peace among ourselves and with all nations."

Lincoln lived to make peace, and not war, for his country.

We must pray for guidance to elect prophets as our government leaders. And we have the responsibility to continue to pray for them when they assume the roles which give them control over the destiny of a nation. As we become united in a singleness of purpose we shall have the right to make peace in the world.

He maketh wars to cease unto the end of the earth ; he breaketh the bow, and cutteth the spear in sunder ; he burneth the chariot in the fire. Be still, and know that I am God : I will be exalted among the heathen, I will be exalted in the earth. (Psalm 46 : 9–10)

A Psalm of Gratitude

OUR Father, we worked for Thee till we thought we should become
    weak in Thy service,
      But Thou hast renewed our strength ; we have mounted up with
    wings as eagles.
We gave unto Thee our all
But Thou hast filled our barns with grain.
We gave ourselves utterly to Thee, without stint and without measure,
Only to find ourselves returning to meet ourselves, clad in garments of
    glory.
    We made ourselves completely captive to Thy will,
    And behold, Thou hast set us eternally free ;
    We let Thee have complete dominion over us ;
    And behold, Thou hast given us dominion over every living creature.
How can we ever thank Thee, how can we ever repay Thee, Thou Lord of
    our lives ?
For even the thanks we send forth to Thee upon the wings of the morning
Return bearing gifts in the evening.
All we can do is to continue to give, give, give to the uttermost.
All that we have is Thine ; all that we are is Thine.
Take us, use us, we cannot be exhausted ;
The more we are used the more beautiful, the more eternal, we become.
Thou hast set a Light within our hearts that radiates eternal Love.
And the light of Love shining through the fountain of Life reveals the
    rainbow of Joy,
Joy that is eternal, unending, complete,
The perfect promise of Thy perfect fulfilment.
Accept our thanksgiving, our praise, our gratitude without stint and with-
    out measure, O Father,
For Thine is the Kingdom and the Power and the Glory forever and ever.
                                       Amen.

In the beginning was the Word, and the Word was with God, and the
Word was God. The same was in the beginning with God. All things
were made by him ; and without him was not any thing made that was
made. In him was life ; and the life was the light of men. (John 1 : 1–4)

WHEN one views life from the highest planes he discovers that there is only one Being in all the universe and that one is God; there is only one Love and that comes from the Heart of God; there is only one Time and that is the Eternal Now; there is only one Space and that is the Infinite Here. And finally there is only one Motion and that is the motion of keeping in perfect balance in relation to all of these.

Perfection of any kind is attained when we discover our Centre in God and learn to keep balanced there. When we have only one emotion and that one is Love, filling us so full there is no room for fear, then we know bliss. When we are content in the Now without regrets for the past and without concern for the future, then we have joy. When we are content in the Here without envy or yearning to be elsewhere, then we find peace. In other words when we are content with the motionless motion of resting in the Centre of God's Love Here and Now, then we experience heaven.

And then we do not seek ideas; Love will draw them to us in perfect order and perfect sequence. We do not seek people; Love will draw the right ones to us when we want to be with them. We do not hunt for riches, Love will bring us our daily bread and all else as we need it. When we look carefully at the Lord's Prayer we find in that masterpiece Jesus' instructions for achieving this perfect balance in the Centre of God.

Our Father which art in heaven, Hallowed be thy name. Thy kingdom come. Thy will be done in earth, as it is in heaven. Give us this day our daily bread. And forgive us our debts, as we forgive our debtors. And lead us not into temptation, but deliver us from evil: For thine is the kingdom, and the power, and the glory, for ever. Amen. (Matthew 6 : 9- 13)

A Living Christ

To experience the power of Jesus Christ even for one moment is to experience Him forever. One is never the same again. All fretfulness, triviality and self-importance fall like drops of water from the shaking aspen leaves. Nothing henceforth is without meaning to one who has seen the Christ, for everything henceforth is bathed through and through with the Love of God, partaking of the eternal values of heaven itself.

The touch of Christ has for me (and hence could have for all) changed ashes to roses, restored the wasted years that the locust has eaten, transformed this world of war and hate into a heaven of love. And all because Christ was here in the body, and because He is here in Spirit. We who follow Him, and grow still in the stillness of His presence, may have Him with us now and forever.

Yes, I have returned permanently to Jesus. That is the one Reality I have derived from this precious journey, and that is what I hope you will continue to share with me. For " neither death, nor life, nor angels, nor principalities, nor powers, nor things present, nor things to come, nor height, nor depth, nor any other creature, shall be able to separate us from the love of God, which is in Christ Jesus our Lord " (Romans 8 : 38–39). And everyone who has truly returned to Jesus can verify this. Henceforth let us go up and down the roads of the entire world, proclaiming the good tidings that Jesus is a living Christ, and to-day in this twentieth century He is the most real figure in all the world.

And I have declared unto them thy name, and will declare it : that the love wherewith thou hast loved me may be in them, and I in them. (John 17 : 26)

182

Illustrator's Postscript

IF THE reader has enjoyed the writer's and his pictorial team-mate's joint adventure in moulding words and pictures into this book, perhaps he will be interested to know why I, as an illustrator, feel particularly happy about this experience.

For the first time in my long professional life as a pictorial journalist I have found in Glenn Clark a really understanding partner in trying to express experiences of the spirit through both words and pictures.

Pictures have always appeared to me as particularly suited to capture and transmit reactions of the soul. Such reactions wrapped in emotions are written on the human face. The camera is a marvellous instrument to capture these reflections and create short-cuts between human beings. The pictures can be used as important tools in the crusade for the liberation of the souls of men. The use of such pictures in this book is, I hope, a step toward this goal.

Glenn Clark spoke to you about the " analogy of the stereoscope." May I speak now of another. The atomic fission and the release of the awe-inspiring energies dormant in the nucleus had been possible in theory long before they were accomplished. But not until the advent of the cyclotron was a strong enough bombardment of the nucleus possible to make atomic fission a fact.

There is magic in words and there is magic in pictures. They have done many great things separately. The effect of the two on each other is some-times amazing. Together they create a new power, new momentum, a " cyclotron " to start chain reactions.

It is my hope and prayer that the words and the pictures in this volume through their combined power will create many chain reactions for the release of the divine in human souls.

I am deeply grateful to God for having brought me into touch with Glenn Clark who has seen Him from such a close range ; for having given us publishers who share our vision and helpful friends and advisers whose understanding and prayers have contributed much.

LUCIEN AIGNER

Meditation Sources

Books by Glenn Clark

AT present only *I Will Lift Up Mine Eyes*, 12s. post free, *The Soul's Sincere Desire*, 9s. post free, and *How to Find Health Through Prayer*, 11s. post free, are available in Great Britain. However, the publishers plan to produce other Glenn Clark titles in the near future.

Notes on Photographs

The location of some of the photographs is indicated below :

Photographs taken at Camps Farthest Out :

Photograph Acknowledgments

Syd Berry : photograph facing page 106
Glenn Clark (private collection) : photographs facing pages 62, 132, 134, 146
Great Northern Railway : photographs facing pages 20, 136, 172
G. D. Hackett : photographs facing pages 42, 58, 86, 94, 180
New York State Pix : photographs facing pages 50, 72
Schall-Pix : photographs facing pages 16, 122, 126
W. Suschitzki-Pix, Inc. : photographs facing pages 80, 156

All other photographs by Lucien Aigner